THE RIVER UNDERGROUND

JEAN TARDIEU

THE RIVER UNDERGROUND

Selected Poems & Prose

Translated by
DAVID KELLEY

BLOODAXE BOOKS

ISBN: 978 1 85224 099 8

First published 1991 by
Bloodaxe Books Ltd,
Eastburn,
South Park,
Hexham,
Northumberland NE46 1BS.

www.bloodaxebooks.com
For further information about Bloodaxe titles
please visit our website and join our mailing list
or write to the above address for a catalogue.

Supported by
ARTS COUNCIL
ENGLAND

Typesetting by EMS Phototypesetting, Spitttal, Berwick-upon-Tweed.

Digital reprint of the 1991 Bloodaxe Books edition.

CONTENTS

Acknowledgements

Acknowledgements are due to the following publishers for permission to reprint poems and prose by Jean Tardieu in this book: Éditions de la Pléiade for work from *Le fleuve caché* (1933); Éditions de Grenelle for *Les figures du mouvement* (1987); and Éditions Gallimard for *Le témoin invisible* (1943), *Figures* (1944), *Jours pétrifiés* (1947), *Monsieur Monsieur* (1951), *Une voix sans personne* (1954), *L'espace et la flûte* (1958), *Histoires obscures* (1961), *La part de l'ombre* (1972), *Formeries* (1976), *Comme ceci comme cela* (1979) and *Les tours de Trébizonde* (1983). The texts used for Tardieu's Gallimard volumes are those in the *Poésies*/Gallimard series: *Le fleuve caché: Poésies 1938-1961* (1968) and *L'accent grave et l'accent aigu: Poèmes 1976-1983* (1986). 'La mouche et l'océan', written in 1910/11, is published in the first section of this book corresponding to *Le fleuve caché* (1933), but was first collected in *Margeries* (Gallimard, 1986).

The text of 'Grilles et balcons' (from *La part de l'ombre*) also exists in a different version, published under the name Jean Ceyzériat in *Europe* no. 144 (15 December 1934).

Bloodaxe Books Ltd and David Kelley wish to thank the Ministère de la Culture, Paris, and Trinity College, Cambridge, for help given towards production and translation costs.

The cover painting was photographed by Jean-Louis Viossat.

Jean Tardieu

According to Baudelaire, the most important events in the life of a great artist occur 'beneath the sky which is the skull'. Jean Tardieu would, I suspect, agree with this, since, at the end of the chronology of his life he provided me with for this biographical sketch, he notes that it is the summary of a full life, but one filled with work rather than events. And yet this might give a false impression. He is anything but a dried-up intellectual. At the age of eighty-six he still exudes a physical vitality, and shows an enthusiasm for the good things in life – friends, food, wine and beautiful women – which may, superficially, seem out of key with the metaphysical anxiety which is at the centre of his work. A friend's affectionate nickname for him is 'the fat ferret', and this sums him up. He is simultaneously a fat man with a thin man trying to get out, and a thin man from whom a fat man has managed to emerge.

Jean Tardieu was born in 1903, in Saint-Germain-de-Joux, a small village in the French Jura. His father, Victor Tardieu, was a successful painter, influenced by the Post-Impressionists, but producing large-scale representations of working-class life (dock-yard scenes set in Paris, London, Liverpool and Genoa), and huge decorative ceilings for town halls in the suburbs of Paris. His mother, Caroline, but always known as Câline, was a musician, and the importance of these two artistic influences is discussed in my introduction to his work.

In 1904 the family moved to Paris, where they led a well-to-do life in a two-floor apartment in the rue Chaptal, at the foot of Montmartre. Tardieu recounts having been brought up as a rich *bourgeois*, under the influence of a rich godmother who took him for rides in her carriage in the Bois de Boulogne on Sunday afternoons, like a character out of Proust. The summers were spent in his grandparents' house in the countryside near Lyon – and particularly in the garden, the garden in which he is depicted, with his mother, in the cover illustration to this book – which he remembers as a kind of lost paradise.

But however idyllic this Proustian and Impressionist childhood might seem, Tardieu's early memories are not entirely happy ones. Even as a child he was turned in upon himself, sensing, particularly at nightfall, invisible, disquieting presences, and remembers posing

himself banal, unanswerable, philosophical questions, in the style of: 'The earth moves round the sun, the sun is in the sky, but what is the sky in?'

In any case, the idyll was to be destroyed by the outbreak of war in September 1914. Victor Tardieu joined up for the duration, and Jean and his mother lived alone together in Paris in reduced circumstances, on the money his mother earned by teaching the harp – mainly to enticing young girls who excited the adolescent poet's desires, although, from what he says in *Margeries* (Margeries), his actual experience seems at this point to have been limited to notes slipped from hand to hand and the odd furtive kiss. He was, however, quite precocious, since his first experience of erotic passion, also described in *Margeries*, occurred in 1919 and involved a married woman – a young provincial with whom he engaged in an intense correspondence, and whom he planned to meet, only to be foiled by his parents who intercepted one of the letters and cut everything short for fear of scandal.

The same period also saw his tentative début as a dramatist. During one of his father's periods of leave from the front, he was taken to see Molière's *Le malade imaginaire* at the Comédie Française, which resulted in his writing a parody of a literature class at school which he called *Le magister malgré lui*.

In his final year at the *lycée* Condorcet, 1920, he went through a severe mental crisis. This was triggered off by looking at himself in the mirror one day while shaving, and becoming terrified at the sight of his "double" – and perhaps this is relevant to a reading of the peom 'Incarnation'. He had to postpone taking the *baccalauréat*, and spent his time instead writing rather pessimistic poetry and prose.

But through a school-friend, Jacques Heurgon, he met Paul Desjardins who had just set up a summer seminar in a Romanesque abbey near Laroche in Burgundy, where Tardieu met the European intelligentsia of the time: Gide, Rivière, Schlumberger, Unamuno, Leon Chestov, Lytton Strachey, and Tatyana Tolstoy. And in 1927 his first poems were published in the prestigious magazine *La Nouvelle Revue Française* by Jean Paulhan.

Meanwhile, Tardieu had been finishing a degree in Letters, having switched from Law. He managed to arrange to do his deferred National Service in Hanoi, where his father had been commissioned to set up an art school. As he still seemed to be a weakly young man, he was lucky enough to be excused active service and posted to a desk job with the General Staff, where his

C.O. was the brother of the writer Marcel Aymé. Nevertheless, the colonial atmosphere of Vietnam was uncongenial, and his life there was ill-matched to his political principles. He spent three weeks in the glasshouse for visiting young Vietnamese revolutionary poets on Sundays. The enormous consolation was meeting Marie-Laure Blot, a young scientist just beginning a brilliant career as a botanist, whom he was to marry in 1932, and who was to become Assistant Director of Research at the Jardin des Plantes, and then Director of Research at the École des Hautes Études. Marie-Laure Tardieu is, in her eighties, a woman of enormous beauty, intelligence and charm, who has managed to combine being an extremely distinguished scientist in her own right with being the archivist and promoter of her poet husband.

In 1932 he returned to Paris, where he worked for the Musées nationaux, and then for the weekly, *Toute l'édition*. In 1933, he published, in the review *Mesures*, a translation of Friedrich Hölderlin's poem 'The Archipelago', and also his first collection of poetry, *The River Underground*.

His collection of poems, *Accents*, was published by Gallimard just before the outbreak of war, in 1939. He was called up to a desk job in Paris, and then demobilised, spending the duration of the war in the capital, with his family (a daughter, Alix-Laurence had been born in 1936). But he became actively engaged with the literary Resistance, giving work to clandestine magazines and publishers (L'honneur des Poètes, Les Éditions de Minuit, Fontaine, etc), and got to know other Resistance writers: Aragon, Éluard, Seghers, Queneau, Lucian Scheler, Henri Thomas, and above all André Frénaud, with whom he entered into a close friendship – they were known as the two dolphins because neither of them had managed to learn to swim.

After the liberation of Paris, in 1944, he was appointed Head of the Drama Department of French Radio. And in 1946, he was asked to set up a *Club d'essai* for French radio and television, the function of which was to engage in experimental radio productions. This brought him into contact with celebrities like Claudel, Braque, Jean-Louis Barrault, Darius Milhaud, Honegger and Bachelard, but also gave him the chance of helping open the door to talented young people like François Billetdoux, Gilbert Amy, Michel Polac, Jean Négroni and Jean Topart.

At the same time, he was publishing, as well as *Les dieux étouffés*, a collection of clandestine poems written during the war years, and *Jours pétrifiés* (1947), the first attempts at a new form of dramatic

11

writing, the short scenic poems '*Qui est là?*' and '*La politesse inutile*'. And in 1949 he began to gain recognition as a dramatist with the production, by René Guiette, of *Qui est là?* and the performance, by Agnès Capri with Michel de Ré, of the comic sketch *Un mot pour un autre*, which was to have a lasting success. In the coming years, this reputation was to grow, and Tardieu's work in this field was to be linked with the names of Beckett and Ionesco as an example of the so-called Theatre of the Absurd.

Tardieu is quite reticent about the remainder of his life up to the present. The chronological notes he has provided me with become above all a list of publications. He notes the marriage of his daughter, Alix, to Giuseppe Baudo, an Italian chemical engineer in 1963; and the birth of his first grandson, Nicolas Baudo, in 1969; her divorce and remarriage to a Milanese lawyer, Giovanni Turolla in 1975; and the birth of a second grandson, Giacomo Turolla, in 1976. His mother, Câline, died, aged 94, in 1968. With characteristic understatement, he mentions briefly that, with the composer Marius Constant, he was responsible for setting up a new radio station which was to become France-Musique.

He retired from the ORTF in 1969, and Marie-Laure retired from her post at the École des Hautes Études in 1972. For the past two decades, in spite of the demands of his work for radio and television, Tardieu had been regularly publishing volumes of prose, theatre, poetry and texts on music and the visual arts. Retirement did not in any way interrupt his literary activity. On the contrary, it has given him more time to devote to writing, and to the re-editing of earlier works, so that the years since 1969 have seen a constant flow of essays, poetry and theatre. His most recent work, the biographical reminiscences, *On vient chercher Monsieur Jean*, was published by Gallimard in 1990, and only the other day he expressed the hope that he would live long enough to finish the long play he has been planning for some years.

I don't think he has to worry. As Théophile Gautier once said of Delacroix, Jean Tardieu and Marie-Laure will die young at the age of a hundred. In spite of the ill-health associated with age, both of them continue to travel to give readings and lectures and to attend conferences and colloquia. In their flat in Paris (the fifth floor aquarium of 'The Towers of Trebizond'), in their house in Gerberoy near Beauvais, in their other house in Italy, they offer warmth, encouragement, wit, intelligence, good food and good wine – as well as a perfectly lethal *marc* from Jean's home region, the Jura – to friends, younger poets, actors, directors, translators

and academics. It may be that, like Mallarmé's Poe, Jean Tardieu will eventually be transformed into an ideal version of himself defined by his writing, but for me that ideal image of Jean Tardieu will always be accompanied by a vision of the 'fat ferret', fork poised, eyes, ears and nose alerted.

Introduction

The first poem in this book was written when Jean Tardieu was seven or eight years old (his age in the cover picture). It is the kind of poem many of us wrote at primary school, when our parents would fondly imagine they could see signs of precocious genius in the naive scribblings of their offspring, and might almost justify that outdated critical method of trying to discern in the artist's origins the seeds of his mature work. Yet in Tardieu's case these clichés have some basis. For in this brief poem are contained both the most important influences on his writing and what critics have seen as being its contradictory aspects.

On a primary level, these influences were his father and his mother – as noted in the biographical sketch, the one a successful painter, the other a musician. And Tardieu has said that if he took up writing it was because, intimidated by their skill in what they did, he wanted to find something that he could do better. On a secondary level, however, the parents were also important. For at bedtime his father would read him Hugo, Baudelaire and Verlaine, and his mother, La Fontaine.

'The Fly and the Ocean' is too slight and too childish a poem to bear the weight of much critical exegesis, but it does bring together those two strands. On the one hand, the metaphysical pretensions of Victor Hugo, on the other the humour of La Fontaine. What is remarkable is that at that early age, Jean Tardieu seems to have grasped the most important features of the art of both poets. In the fly winging above the ocean is encapsulated that play between the minute and the enormous which most clearly characterises the cosmic vision of Hugo. In the facetious moral tag which concludes the poem is summarised the wit of La Fontaine, which has constantly to undermine the surface didacticism of his Fables, and enlarge its import. The assimilation of both elements within the space of five lines is, at the very least, extremely clever.

The influence of Hugo is an all-pervading one in modern French poetry. Hugo's poetry involves a quite remarkable quality of vision – recognised by Rimbaud in his *Lettres du Voyant*. But it also involves a rhetorical pomposity which even the Surrealists never managed completely to throw off. And Tardieu is no exception. The Hugolian legacy is to be found, in the form which is perhaps

most alien to the English ear, and most recalcitrant to the translator, in the rhetoric of certain lines of poems like 'Incarnation' and 'The River Underground'. But in Tardieu metaphysical anxiety is never simply rhetorical, although it is often intimately connected with problems of language. Its roots are most clearly expressed in the introduction to his series of prose and verse poems dealing with painting and music, *Les portes de toile* (Gates of Canvas):

> In a world in which all is silent and subject to the threat of a horrifying absence, man, who in former times was lulled by the voice of the gods, discovers himself to be alone, obliged to take up the challenge thrown down by the obscure powers of destruction, and to reconstruct his own image from the last steps of the void.
>
> He must take responsibility for everything that exists, as though he were its creator, or at least its curator. It is indeed as though, at his approach, even before a word has been spoken, a kind of strange unformed language were to awaken in sounds, in colours and in visible forms. The cruel and touching clumsiness of the universe has long been awaiting his arrival for guidance, for instruction, perhaps for redemption, at the least for deliverance, from its tragic solitude and inability to communicate.

This passage recalls a text which might have been written by Hugo, but which in fact comes from one of the other nineteenth-century poets read to Tardieu by his father, Baudelaire, who perceives the 'visible universe' as:

> a store of images and signs to which the imagination will give a relative place and value; it is a kind of pasture which the imagination has to digest and transform. ['Salon de 1859']

And indeed I am tempted to see in the 'strange unformed language' wakening in 'sounds, colours and visible forms' an echo of the 'confused words' and the intermingling of sounds, colours and perfumes of Baudelaire's sonnet *'Correspondances'*, that manifesto of the poetic revolution of the nineteenth and early twentieth centuries.

In the Tardieu text, as Baudelaire's, the world is a 'store of images and signs', waiting on man, the only being capable of lending them meaning and sense. But for Tardieu, writing a hundred years later than Hugo and Baudelaire, and no longer seriously believing in the quasi-mystical notion of the *'imagination'* which is central to Baudelaire's theory of metaphor based on *'correspondences'*, the artist who gives meaning to the universe is less confident of being an *avatar* of the Creator. The role of the artist – and with Tardieu the artist is always involved in play, and often in playing a role – is rather that of the grudging intendant of an

absentee-landlord, forced, against his better judgement, to take up the challenge thrown down by the obscure forces of the void which constantly threaten the estate.

In this, his position is closer to that of a Camus – who thought very highly of 'Incarnation' – than that of Hugo or Baudelaire. For Camus the 'plague' of the novel by the same title is at once a symbol of 'the absurd', and of the Nazi occupation which is its (in)human manifestation. The same might be said of the 'crushing enemy of man' to which Tardieu refers in his introduction to *Les portes de toile.*

Indeed, Tardieu has himself said on many occasions that he began writing the texts which make up that volume – of which the 'Cézanne' included in this selection is an excellent example – at the darkest moment of the war, when many of the paintings from the national collections had been removed for safety or stolen by the Germans, in order to create for himself a kind of verbal and mental museum safe from the ravages of the events of the period. And some of the verse poems in this book, notably 'The Stifled Gods', reflect Tardieu's response to the alliance of man's inhumanity to man with the obscure forces of the void represented by the Occupation.

But Francis Ponge – a close friend of Tardieu and a former colleague, since they worked together for Hachette in the pre-war years – criticised Camus' *Myth of Sisyphus* for failing to come to grips with the importance of language in the problem of the absurd as he posed it – that is as the irreductibility of the universe to man's attempts to make sense of it. But for Tardieu the problems of language are central. The 'strange unformed language' referred to by Tardieu corresponds very closely to his own preoccupations. In *Obscurité du jour* (Daylight Darkness) he talks of an *'en-deçà du Sens'* – what lies beneath meaning:

> I began this book by trying to imagine, as opposite extremes, what is *beneath* Meaning and what is *beyond* Meaning.
>
> Beneath Meaning, for example, was that enigmatic and disturbing noise made by words, a rumbling which had no meaning of itself (except for a few imitative sounds), but which, supposing that I did not speak the language spoken around me, could nevertheless serve as an instinctive signal, on an emotional level, by the *tone* of voice.
>
> And I added: 'I cannot speak to a human being through a door which masks his words, without being seized by an unbearable anxiety.'
>
> Beyond Meaning, I could see nothing but the vagueness of what is uncertain and doubtful, but this fog was boundless, for it contains everything that, in times past, it was thought seemly to define that awful word "ineffable", which finally is but the infinite possibility of language.

That other extreme of meaning, 'beyond Meaning' is presumably the transcendental function of language sought, in different ways, by Baudelaire, Rimbaud and Mallarmé – a transcendental function which is of course impossible, since language is both human and finite. And it is the fact that these poets both recognised and refused this which gives a dramatic tension to their poetry.

Tardieu has rather more limited claims. Accepting that the "ineffable" is unattainable, and that it is 'difficult, if not impossible, to separate words from their meaning', he seeks what he refers to as an 'oscillation':

> Just as everything that lives oscillates between a perpetual birth and a perpetual death, that which moves in language when it seeks to be "other", oscillates between usage and derangement, between form and content, between will and chance, between sense and non-sense.

That is to say that he engages in a conscious play within that ambiguous space which exists between what seeks meaning – the virtual signifier, which in order to accede to the status of sign, longs for a signified – and what, having sought liberation from the signified to reach the status of pure signifier, arrives at the void.

It is for this reason that, in 'Grilles and Balconies', he is fascinated by the delicate wrought-ironwork of the balconies of Paris apartment buildings. On the one hand, as simple components of the urban decor they seem to be 'beneath Meaning', a kind of visual noise seeking to be deciphered, engaging the eye in the constant human urge to decipher, to create meaning:

> Everything which is *inscribed* fascinates our gaze: the lode in a rock, the trace left in the skin of a fruit by the gnawing of a worm, the veins in a leaf, the light on the edge of a hill.

On the other hand, they are the product of human artistry, complex abstract structures in space, figures of a language so pure that it requires no specific or precise signified – therefore, in Tardieu's terms a language 'beyond Meaning'. Defining space while yet creating space, inviting reading while refusing to impose a reading, they are 'proof against error':

> Let us recall to our grateful minds those charmers of iron who fashioned with flame a language so perfect that they never even felt the need to impose on it a particular "sense". Eternally indecipherable, these cyphers are proof against error.

The greater part of Tardieu's work consists of various forms of play within these two poles, between what is beneath meaning and what is beyond meaning – play in the sense of the play in a machine, as in 'Grilles and Balconies', where the definitions of the

status of sign are both precise and fluidly intangible, where the poles are both exact and interchangeable.

It also involves play in the ludic sense: a sense of fun, a play with language almost in the sense in which children play with building blocks. As, for example, in texts from *Formeries* like 'Sounds in S', in which one set of words beginning with "s" is given a privileged position, and another set swept to the corner of the page in a heap. This kind of play with language may seem childlike, if not childish, compared with the extremely complex linguistic games played by Ponge, for example.

Yet Tardieu's apparently simple game works in a not dissimilar way to that of Ponge, who, in a text like *'Le gymnaste'* (The Acrobat), plays with actual shape of the letters which make up the word – the bar and serif of the G for example correspond to the mustachio and beard of the conventional circus acrobat – suggesting in a hyperbolically absurd way that there is some necessary relationship between the signifier and the signified, and thus pushing the reader into an examination of his or her assumptions about language and its relationship with the outside world.

Tardieu's 'Sounds in S' plays on words as an abstract system, almost like that of music (with S as key), since the sole reason for their being in the text appears to be that they begin with the letter S. He could equally well have chosen D or T. And yet this arbitrary – in terms of the signifying function of language – choice is doubled by another choice. Some words – *Savour, Severity, Suspiration, Sojourn, Secret, Soot* – are privileged – whereas others are rejected to a heap at the bottom of the page: *Sun, Suffering, Serpent, Sarcophagus, Socrates, Samson, Sisyphus,* and so on. This division of sounds in S could of course be determined simply by the acoustic qualities of the signifier – and there is, in the privileged words at least, the vestige of alliterative and assonantal sound patterns.

But the 'sounds' which constitute the text are not simply sounds – as in some Futurist or Dadaist poems – but words. The reader is thus invited to find some reason on the level of signification for the separation of the words into two categories. With some, it is obvious. *Savour* and *Suspiration* are positive – *Suffering, Serpent* and *Sarcophagus,* negative. But why should *Severity* and *Soot* be privileged, and *Sun, Socrates* and *Sisyphus* be relegated to the pile at the bottom of the page?

The fact that *Soot* follows *Secret* helps perhaps, since, to some extent at least, it defines the semantic resonance of the word. The softness and darkness of soot can be perceived as positive qualities

in the context in which the word is situated. And this helps perhaps to suggest reasons why *Sun, Socrates* and *Sisyphus* should be demoted. Positive value is given to intimate depths and darkness – one of Tardieu's volumes is entitled *La part de l'ombre* (The Shadow's Share) – as opposed to the brilliance of the sun and philosophy and the heroic struggle against the absurd of Camus' Sisyphus. But this jars, in an ambiguous way, with the previous frame of reference, and a complex and intriguing play between abstract sound patterns and the semantic field of the words, one which is wittily amusing, but which also has profoundly disturbing uncertainties at its centre.

The collection *Monsieur Monsieur* unites play in the ludic sense with play in the dramatic sense. Tardieu is a well-known dramatist in France, and was writing short plays which combine wit and humour with anguished metaphysical speculation in the mode of what has become known as the Theatre of the Absurd at the same time as, if not before, Ionesco and Beckett. (His first experiments in writing for the theatre, *Qui est là?* (Who's there?) and *La politesse inutile* (Unnecessary politeness) were published in 1946.) Space restrictions have prevented the inclusion of any of the plays in this book, but the *Monsieur Monsieur* texts offer a suggestion of the atmosphere of Tardieu's theatrical work as well as an indication of the ways in which a certain kind of lyricism contains within it the germ of drama. (In this Tardieu follows in the tradition of Musset.)

The argument which precedes the *Monsieur Monsieur* poems makes the latter point evident:

> The action takes place at the intersection between the Lyric and the Burlesque (it was cold and the scarecrow's rags were flapping in the winds of space), here on this flea-pit puppet theatre there will shortly appear two identical gentlemen, each of whom is but the shadow of the other, ham actors playing at philosophy, elements of eternity reduced to the proportions of the absurd, truth and sincerity acted out by parodies of themselves – here it was I hid to write these poems.

The 'two identical gentlemen, each of whom is but the shadow of the other' are clearly elements of a fractured lyrical voice – as is emphasised by the remark 'here it was I hid to write these poems'. Indeed, Tardieu claims that the idea for the title of the volume and for the poems derives from the nineteenth-century manner of addressing letters 'A Monsieur, Monsieur Un Tel', which is equivalent to our English practice of addressing a letter to Mr So and So and beginning the letter: Dear Sir. In both cases the two forms of address refer to the same person, but the specificity of that

person somehow evaporates under the formal impersonality of the mode of address.

The dialogues which constitute the *Monsieur Monsieur* poems thus represent a kind of dramatic lyricism which expresses the extremely problematic nature of lyricism. The "self" which seeks to express itself is distanced and dispersed by the splitting off into two anonymous voices. Expression is a form of concealment: 'here it was I hid to write these poems'. The metaphysical anxiety which is a constant in Tardieu's poetry discovers itself to be so banal that it cannot find the courage of its convictions in order to define itself as feeling or felt.

That is the essence of the problem of lyricism since the Romantic period. It is the dilemma of Musset, the prematurely disillusioned idealist who, in plays like *Fantasio* or *On ne badine pas avec l'amour*, projects, with subtle irony, the profound contradictions that in most of his lyric poetry emerge as sententious and sentimental, into multiple voices. It is also perhaps the dilemma of Artaud, who perceived in the situation of the actor (who both plays a role and finds expression in action), the means to a naive and innocent language. It is certainly the dilemma of Beckett, who creates out of the apparently incoherent parody of intelligence which is the dialogue between the Didi and Gogo of *Waiting for Godot* a lyricism of silence.

Indeed, the pompously grotesque exchanges of, for example, 'Mister Sir at the Seaside' have much in common with the so-called Theatre of the Absurd of *Waiting for Godot* – not least the evaporation of the non-characters who have been trying to solve the problems of the universe:

> At these words the wind comes up
> and blows away their hats
> and the two figures
> evaporate
> into the clear blue sky.

Yet however anguished Tardieu's world view may be, his humour is less bleak and less black than Beckett's. It contains an element of childlike and even – in a positive sense – childish sense of fun which is lacking in the Irish writer. The seven year old of 'The Fly and the Ocean' is still present in the mature poet of 'Ragamuffin Nuffin' ', which, in a parody of the dramatic mode, poses the problem of the possible or probable non-existence of any divine absolute as a childish joke.

But the relationship between Tardieu's lyricism and his sense of theatre is perhaps most explicit in the long prose poem 'My Secret

Theatre'. For here Tardieu evokes his inner world in terms of a theatre, inviting us to admire the perfect presentation or representation which is constituted by his work, but also letting us behind the scenes, to see the tawdry scaffolding and snaking electric cables which enable the show to go on – the clichéd scraps of culture, from Shakespeare's Lady Macbeth and Watteau's *Gilles* to nineteenth-century melodrama and Charlie Chaplin which make up the mental universe "dramatised" in the poetry and plays. And discreet allusions to his own dramatic works emphasise this relationship: the keyhole and the ticket office among the props he manages to slip into the theatre under the nose of the Financial Director and the technicians.

I have already noted the importance of Tardieu's musician mother and painter father in his own artistic development, and I have referred to *Les portes de toile*, written in the dark days of the Second World War, in which he attempted, in a style half-way between criticism and the prose poem, to create a kind of verbal museum and record library of the major works of French music and painting. His poems and plays consistently refer to music and painting, and play with the structures of music or the visual arts. An excellent example of this is *Space and the Flute*, which is a kind of *transposition d'art* of the kind of which Théophile Gautier was a master, an evocation of and commentary on line drawings by Picasso referring to and commenting on music.

This has led some commentators to assume that Tardieu is fundamentally envious of musicians and painters for the materials of their art. Some texts would seem to bear this out, as for example in *Space and the Flute*, where he writes:

> One day thus shall I wind around things
> a ribbon proffered by the voice
> a single unending perfect docile word.

These lines clearly refer to the technique which Picasso uses in the drawings, which combine extreme simplicity with extraordinary sophistication, and indeed often do encapsulate objects and figures in a single, supple, seemingly perfect, unbroken line.

Equally clearly, Tardieu is perfectly aware that the desire he expresses is an impossible one. One of the fundamental character-istics of language is that it is composed of discrete units, which cannot pass a ribbon around things. Another is the Saussurian principle of the arbitrary nature of the sign. There is no necessary relationship between signifier and signified. But if the means at the disposal of the painter also constitute a relative signifying system –

in which perspective is an obvious element – the ways in which the painter or the draughtsman's image relate to objects in the outside world is different from and less arbitrary than those which operate in spoken or written language.

In fact these lines are a witty conceit, the purpose of which is more to validate the writer's art than to deprecate it. Indeed, Tardieu has this in common with Gautier, that his profound and intimate knowledge of other art forms has led him to reflect with more than usual intelligence on the specific qualities of his own medium. If he takes as starting point a work of music or painting, it is not so much with the desire to imitate it, as with the aim of working out the possibilities of writing.

In particular, both music and painting represent for him areas in which the writer can play within the space which is defined by the poles 'beneath Meaning' and 'beyond Meaning'. Music is 'beneath Meaning' in so far as the sounds which constitute it have no identifiable signified. But it can also be thought to be 'beyond Meaning' in constituting a system which, to quote Beckett, 'makes shape of the mess', without needing to have any specific meaning. And the short plays like *Concert sinfonietta*, in which conversation is structured according to the conventions of music, work in precisely this way. Language is simultaneously banalised and transcendentalised. The formal structures of music applied to conversation both emphasise the emptiness of conventional social discourse and shape it in a way which transforms that void of meaning into an abstract structure which does not depend on meaning.

This corresponds very closely to Tardieu's fascination with the wrought-ironwork of 'Grilles and Balconies'. And in the texts on painting in *Les portes de toile* a major theme is the ambivalent relationship between concrete representation and abstraction. In the 'Cézanne', for example, he begins with abstraction, but an abstraction that is strangely concrete. For he evokes that perception which is one of Cézanne's most salient characteristics, of the profound relationship between colour – for Delacroix or Monet a means of rendering the fluid evanescence of things – and mass, form, structure, solidity. A relationship which is based on the molecular composition of objects, and which means that colour is 'the magic and moving intersection of the seeing soul and seen presences...' But the poet then particularises this definition of the role of colour in the perception of forms and objects by discreet and allusive reference to known themes and paintings of the painter – and particularly to that almost obsessive motif in Cézanne, the

Montagne Sainte-Victoire:

> Then, in the spaces between the touches of colour, there are no more than faceless gaps, no more than the void. And yet, manifestly, the mountain still stands.

These lines suggest, however, the purpose of Tardieu's interrogation of the work of Cézanne. Through his words as much as through the paint-strokes of Cézanne, the meaning of the mountain and the paintings comes through. It is precisely because the mountain still stands, 'on the transparent leaf of the stretched surface', that the universe still stands; because of that transparency, marked by traces of paint and ink, that everything stands. It is perhaps no accident that the mountain's name is Sainte-Victoire (Sacred Victory).

A similar process is at work in 'The Towers of Trebizond', which plays off the image of the tower blocks of the Porte d'Italie on the southern perimeter of Paris against the complex tower images which occupy the background of the fresco by Pisanello representing the struggle between St George and the dragon.

Here too, it is from the play between abstraction and the concrete (literally), that the poet moves towards meaning. The tower blocks, brute reality, deriving from a brutalist aesthetic, are nevertheless human in that they seem to be attempting to send out signals. The lights in the windows, switched on or switched off relentlessly but irregularly, suggest some 'enigmatic Morse code'. A language which is 'beneath Meaning', in that its system is random – yet is created nevertheless by human beings – it implores, like the traceries of the balconies, a reading of kinds.

The scene evoked in the second half of the text, the Pisanello fresco, is enigmatic in a very different way, both from the tower blocks of semi-suburban Paris and from abstract painting or music. It is mysterious above all because it appears overcharged with meaning. Or rather because the artist appears to be caught between two rival demands, 'concern for precise naturalistic truth which characterises the beginning of the Renaissance and an already outdated nostalgia for Medieval fable' and to have 'wanted to slip into our hand the lost key to those symbols whose secret is perhaps their capacity to make us re-live "on demand" the unchanging yet constantly renewed phases of a magic and sacred ritual'. It is a work of art which seems both to offer and refuse an opening onto what is 'beyond Meaning' by the solid materiality of the figures in the painting and by their enigmatic significative density.

And in fact, in Tardieu's evocation of the painting there is

nothing overtly pointing to any transcendental meaning. In order to suggest the 'stupor comparable to that feeling of anguished anticipation that we sense in face of an approaching storm', he concentrates on the painterly qualities of the work, and particularly on its sumptuously muted colours. Moreover, in interpreting the picture, he makes no attempt, as might an academic art historian, to rediscover 'the lost key' to its symbols. On the contrary, he is content to interrogate the fresco as though it were a play performed in a foreign language, or an episode in a silent film. He describes minutely the postures and expressions of the principal figures in their complex ambiguity. And the ship, the hanged men, the Emperor and his court, bit-part actors in this drama, to which and to whom it is difficult to assign a meaning, are evoked in their enigmatic presence.

But all this acquires a meaning, by reference to the tower blocks of the Porte d'Italie. The blocks are prison-hulks built to devour thousands and thousands of innocent captives, and the victims of the monster slain by St George are described in the following terms:

> It proffers its fearsome muzzle, suggested rather than defined, doubtless still relishing the taste of life at the point of death. Never before has there been such an extreme expression of the contrast between the devastating horror which is the law of the living world and the beauty of the designated victims, that incorruptible and unattainable beauty which is but the reflection of our wearied desires, the supreme court of our despair, and which yet manages to raise itself to the level of a victorious final judgement with no compensation for loss.

A little further on this relationship is made explicit:

> Here it is, in this place of metamorphoses, between yesterday, today and forever, here it is for the benefit of that somnambulism, sometimes ecstatic, sometimes horrified, which saves me, and of those inexplicable apparitions which enchant me, that the towers of Trebizond and those, so aptly named, of the Place d'Italie came to meet.

The mysterious ship of Pisanello's fresco, driven on by the storm, yet frozen by the image of which it is part, meets the motionless fleet of tower blocks; the victims of the dragon are assimilated to the inhabitants of the council estate prison-hulks. But the hero's sadness, the fraternal melancholy of the horse, the 'feigned indifference of the victim', also recall the poet's 'painful and pensive slowness'. His remarks about the beehive cells of the tower blocks might give the impression that he is being condescending. But the apartment from which he looks out on the towers of the Porte d'Italie is also a prison. He describes it as an aquarium, from which, like a fish caught in a lobster pot, he slowly

twists and turns, separated from the boulevard by a glass screen which encloses him, and yet which also functions as a frame defining the image of the tower blocks of the Porte d'Italie, and thus makes of them a picture.

So the poet is both chosen victim and St George killing the monster. The strictly provisional victory is that of reading and writing. That victory consists in reading both the obscure visual data proffered by the Paris tower blocks, potential signs, and the overcharged signs of the Pisanello fresco, and bringing them together in a single texture, that of writing. This is the power of language as against the resources of the painter or the musician – that the writer can play or work within the wasteland which exists between what is 'beneath Meaning' and what is 'beyond Meaning'. If this tiny victory over the 'crushing enemy of mankind' remains provisional, it is because the meaning which the writer attempts to set up in opposition to the void and the darkness is in no way transcendent. It remains strictly human. It is even more precarious than Cézanne's mountain. It is made up of light brushstrokes. It is full of holes. But it 'still stands'. And in the fresco by Pisanello described by Tardieu there is also a glimpse of a mountain, the meaning of which remains unexplained ('beyond the murky sea and the pale blue sky you can half-glimpse the sombre form of a mountain...'). Is it not possible to see in these murky waters Tardieu's 'beneath Meaning', in the pale blue sky what is 'beyond Meaning', and in the mountain, scarcely glimpsed, in parentheses, a 'sacred victory' on the part of the writer?

DAVID KELLEY
Paris and Cambridge, 1990

THE RIVER UNDERGROUND
LE FLEUVE CACHÉ
(1933)

La mouche et l'océan

Une mouche se balançait
Au-dessus d'un océan.
Tout à coup elle se sentit
Prise dans du froid.

Moralité

Il faut toujours faire attention.

[Paris, 1910 ou 1911]

The Fly and the Ocean

A fly swayed
Above an ocean.
Suddenly it felt
Caught up in the cold.

Moral:
Always pay attention.

[Paris, 1910/11]

Le fleuve caché

Pièges de la lumière et de l'ombre sur l'âme,
Jeux et rivalités de tout ce qui paraît,

Regards de la douleur et de l'amour, ô flammes
Immenses que fait naître et mourir un reflet,

Tout un monde appuyé sur un souffle qui chante,
Tout le ciel qui s'écroule au fond d'une eau dormante,

Le désir qui défait les clôtures du temps,
Les désastres lancés au gré de la parole,

Partout le plus pesant soumis à ce qui vole
Et l'immédiat, souverain maître des vivants!

Mais parfois notre esprit, fatigué de l'espace,
S'arrête et peut entendre, après plus d'un détour,

Un vaste grondement égal et bas qui passe
A l'infini, roulant sous les jours UN seul jour.

Plus près que notre cœur mais plus loin que la terre,
Comme du fond d'un gouffre, à travers mille échos,

Au vent du souvenir nous parvient le tonnerre
D'un lourd fleuve en rumeur sous l'arbre et sous l'oiseau.

The River Underground

Traps of light and shade upon the soul,
All appearance plays and plays against,

Regards of pain and love, enormous flames
Giving birth and death to one reflection

A whole world built upon a breath of song
The whole sky sunk beneath a stagnant pool,

Desire undoing the enclosures of time,
Disasters launched at the whim of words,

Weightiest subject always to the fleeting,
Immediate, sovereign master of the living!

But sometimes our mind, grown weary of space,
Stops and gives ear, after many a long detour,

To a huge, low, monotonous rumbling, passing
To the infinite, rolling under the days ONE single day.

Nearer than our heart but further than the earth
Echoing as though from the depths of an abyss,

Comes rumbling, on the wind of memory, the thunder
Of a sullen stream beneath tree and bird.

THE INVISIBLE WITNESS
LE TÉMOIN INVISIBLE
(1943)

Les jours

Dans une ville noire entraînée par le temps
(toute maison d'avance au fil des jours s'écroule)
je rentrais, je sortais avec toutes mes ombres.
Mille soleils montaient comme du fond d'un fleuve,
mille autres descendaient, colorant les hauts murs;
je poursuivais des mains sur le bord des balcons;
des formes pâlissaient (la lumière est sur elles)
ou tombaient dans l'oubli (les rayons ont tourné).
Les jours, les jours…Qui donc soupire et qui m'appelle,
pour quelle fête ou quel supplice ou quel pardon?

Les dieux étouffés

Opacité des murs, silence
tombé sur d'obscures clameurs,
temps où sombre la patience,
soleil de plomb sur la douleur
et les ténèbres de soi-même,
formes de fer, masques de feu,
rochers refermés sur les dieux
ruisselants de pluie et de pleurs,
ouvrez, ouvrez à qui les aime,
ouvrez vos portes dont je meurs!

Days

In a city of darkness caught up in time
(each building crumbles in time before its time).
With all my shadows I went in and went out.
Suns in their thousands rose as from a river bed,
a thousand sunsets coloured the towering walls;
I followed hands on the balconies' edge
forms faded (bearing the brunt of light)
or fell into oblivion (with the turning rays)
Days and days...Who then sighs and who calls,
and to what feast what torture or what pardon?

The Stifled Gods

Opacity of walls silence
fallen on sombre screams
time swallowing patience
leaden sun beating down on pain
on the inner darkness of the self
metallic forms and masks of fire
rocks closed upon the gods
running with rain and with tears,
open open to those who love them,
open your gates for which I die!

Feintes nécessaires

J'appuie et creuse en pensant aux ombres,
je passe et rêve en pensant au roc:

Fidèle au bord des eaux volages
j'aime oublier sur un sol éternel.

Je suis changeant sous les fixes étoiles
mais sous les jours multiples je suis un.

Ce que je tiens me vient de la flamme,
ce qui me fuit se fait pierre et silence.

Je dors pour endormir le jour. Je veille
la nuit, comme un feu sous la cendre…

Ma différence est ma nécessité!
Qui que tu sois, terre ou ciel, je m'oppose,

car je pourchasse un ennemi rebelle
ruse pour ruse et feinte pour feinte!

O châtiment de tant de combats,
O seul abîme ouvert à ma prudence:

Vais-je mourir sans avoir tué l'Autre
qui règne et se tait dans ses profondeurs?

Shams in Need

Thinking of shadows I prop and probe
thinking of granite I flitter and dream:

Faithful beside the flighty waves
on dry eternal land oblivion I seek

Beneath the fixed stars I am change
in the flickering light of day I am one

What I hold firm is born of flame
what evades me turns to stone and silence

I sleep to make the daylight sleep. At night
keep watch like fire beneath the ash...

My difference is my necessity!
come you from heaven or hell I oppose

for I pursue a stubborn foe
trick for trick and sham for sham!

Retribution after so many struggles
only abyss open to my caution

Am I to die before I've killed the Other
who rules and keeps his peace within his depths?

Suite mineure

I

Le ciel est plein de songes mal formés.
Ce grand séjour des êtres refusés
Court menaçant sur ta tête de pierre
et ton nuage monte à la lumière
en te laissant les décombres de tout.

Tu creuses ce qui reste près de nous,
tu reconnais le sol sans complaisance;
un âpre vide étreint chaque présence
et te délivre enfin d'un vain espoir.

Ce sont des mains d'aveugle qui vont voir.

II

Les dieux absents, les morts tout autour,
Les flots confondus, les fleurs en flammes.
L'épaule contre le vent. La marche forcée.
Ne me retenez pas! Quelque chose commence,
Quelque chose se tait, se forme et m'attend.

III

Non, tout cela n'est pas sous le ciel,
Mais dans l'esprit paré pour sa victoire
Où pas un jeu n'est joué sans amour.

IV

Un rêve étonnant m'environne:
je marche en lâchant des oiseaux,
tout ce que je touche est en moi
et j'ai perdu toutes limites.

Suite in Minor Key

I

The sky is filled with ill-formed dreams.
That vast abode of beings refused
Comes threatening upon your stony head
your cloud rises upwards towards the light
leaving you encumbered with the ruins of all.

You probe and furrow what stays close to us,
you recognise the earth without accommodation;
a rasping void embraces every presence,
finally frees you from the vanity of hope.

It's a blind man's hands that are going to see.

II

The absent gods, the surrounding dead,
The mingled waves, the flaming flowers.
Shoulder against the wind. Forced march.
Don't hold me back! Something begins.
Something is silent, takes shape, and waits.

III

No, all that does not exist beneath the sky
Only in the mind adorned for victory
Where games are not played safe for love.

IV

An astounding dream is all about me:
I walk along while freeing birds,
All I touch is there within me
And I have eluded every bound.

V

Quand je passe près d'une ombre
claquant comme un linge au vent
elle souffle à mon regard:
je suis à toi tu me prends
la muraille qui m'enchaîne
m'a préparée pour te plaire.

VI

Sphère de feu flottant sur les ténèbres,
je vais, plus loin que tes bords lumineux,
les yeux fermés rejoindre la nuit pure
et dans mes bras serrer le poids du temps.

VII

De ces soleils que notre nuit tisonne
Cendre, étincelle et demain flamme, feu
le craquement sous le chaume résonne:
total amour sans démons et sans dieux!

VIII

Vois le jour à travers les barreaux
nommés œil, oreille, narine.
Ils te tiennent depuis l'enfance.
Ils sont ta sauvegarde
contre tout ce qui cogne aux parois

mais au-dedans, plus de frontières!
Vole, nage, marche au bras
des formes les plus grandes.
Passe au travers des murs de poudre.
A toi d'assiéger le monde!

IX

Sur la terre où les jours se confondent,
tremblant de revoir une fleur,
j'écrase le sang de mon cœur
dans les dures parois de ce monde.

V

When I pass beside a shadow
flapping like clothes in the wind
it whispers at my glance:
I am yours just take me
the wall which holds me prisoner
prepared me for your pleasure.

VI

Fiery sphere floating on darkness,
beyond your luminous edges I go,
eyes closed, to meet the purity of night
and clasp in my arms the weight of time.

VII

Of those suns stirred by our night
Ash, spark, tomorrow flame, fire
the spluttering sounds beneath the thatch:
total love with no more demons no more gods!

VIII

See daylight through the narrow bars
named eye and ear and nostril.
Since childhood they have held you fast.
They are your only safeguard
against all that beats on walls

but within the frontiers are broken down!
Fly, swim, stride out on the arm
of the largest forms.
Pass at ease through walls of dust.
Yours is the siege of the world.

IX

On the earth where days are mingled,
trembling to see once more a flower,
I crush the very blood of my heart
into the hard walls of this world.

J'abandonne à la nuit les délices
près des bords entrevus les yeux clos;
pour maîtriser le temps qui glisse,
le sable est semé de pavots.

A demain, tendre jour, à demain!
Reste jeune en dormant sous la rive
j'emporte la flamme encor vive
à l'abri de mes fidèles mains.

Voyageur avare et rétif,
le front sur le flot qui s'approche,
je cherche le pays des roches,
des derniers grondements captifs.

X

Ici me vint l'espoir ici la crainte,
ici la certitude et le remords.
O souffles ranimant la flamme éteinte,
quelle fumée aux marges de la mort!

Pour avancer je tourne sur moi-même,
cyclone par l'immobile habité;
de tout éclair j'attends le calme et j'aime
du fond d'un gouffre entrevoir des clartés.

Fleurs! Flammes! Jeux et chants du jour léger,
je puis enfin sourire à vos images:
je n'aurai plus à craindre vos mirages
si je vous vois d'un regard étranger!

XI

La ville en moi fermée, en moi dormant
s'ouvre à la marche. Et les bras vont devant
comme les arbres nus privés de vent.
Mille volets obscurs s'animent du dedans
et le ciel que l'on ne voit pas bouge pourtant.
Quelque chose à travers tout dure longtemps
mais se tait. Serait-il temps, serait-il temps?

I give up to night the delights
glimpsed on the edges with closed eyes;
to master time which slips away,
the sand is sown with opium poppies.

Delicate daylight, I'll see you tomorrow.
Retain your youth asleep beneath the strand
I carry away the ever living flame
sheltered within my faithful hands

Unwilling avaricious traveller,
brow bent over the approaching waves
I seek the region of rocks,
and of the last captive rumblings.

X

Here comes hope and here comes fear,
here certitude and here remorse.
Fire breathed into the extinguished flame,
what smoke on the marches of death!

To advance I turn upon myself,
cyclone invested by stasis;
in lightning's flash await the calm and seek
to glimpse the light within an abyss.

Flowers! Flames! Songs and play of light and day,
at last I can smile at your images:
I shall have nothing to fear from your mirages
if I look upon you with a distant gaze!

XI

The city enclosed within me, sleeping within me
opens to my stride. And my arms go before me
like stripped trees gasping for wind.
Behind a thousand darkened shutters life stirs
and the hidden sky flickers yet with movement.
Throughout it all something is long enduring
yet silent. Could it be time? Could it be time?

XII

Quand j'écoute et n'entends pas,
quand je regarde sans voir,
quand je marche sans un pas,
quand mon soleil devient noir,

je disparais sans mourir,
je vis sans un mouvement.
Nul espoir nul souvenir
dans les forges du moment.

Fondre? Soit, mais pour renaître!
Finir pour recommencer!
Le monde est à reconnaître!
sur les chemins effacés.

XIII

Masque aux yeux morts qui écoute au-dedans,
toujours fidèle à ton commandement.

La flamme de ces flambeaux, renversée,
bouillonne de reflets et de fumée.

Près d'eux! Loin d'eux! Mais les reconnaissant
au front qui tourne, à la main qui se tend.

Plus d'un, déjà favori des ténèbres,
vient-il parfois sur ces pentes funèbres

où sont posés les accidents du jour,
cœurs lumineux, les ombres alentour?

Qu'il soit absous de toute identité
par cette dévorante obscurité!

Qu'il adore les pas qui vont descendre!
Qu'il s'approche en tremblant des fleurs en cendre!

La nuit où fond lentement le soleil
sur chaque objet glisse un secret sommeil.

Ce noir rayon t'élève tout à coup,
triomphant par l'absence à travers tout!

XII

When I listen and cannot hear,
when I look and cannot see,
when I walk without a step,
when my sun is draped in black,

without dying I disappear,
without a movement I live on.
Devoid of hope and memory
in the forges of the moment.

To melt? Yes, but to be reborn!
To end but to begin once more!
The world is there for recognition
on paths which are effaced.

XIII

Mask for dead eyes listening within,
ever faithful to your command.

The downturned flame of these flambeaus,
flickers with reflections and smoke.

Close to them! far from them! But recognising
them by their turning brow, their proffered hand.

Does many a one, favoured by the shades
sometimes venture on these deathly slopes

on which alight the chance effects of daylight,
sunlit hearts with shadows all around?

Let him be absolved of all identity
by that devouring darkness!

Let him adore the footsteps soon to descend!
Let him quivering approach the ashen flowers!

The night where slowly melts the sun
slips over every thing a private sleep.

Abruptly raised aloft by that blackened ray,
by absence you triumph throughout all.

XIV

O vertu des faubourgs, sévérité des rues
que rien ne vient froisser de formes confondues,
vides entre vos rails, gravement retenues
sans sourires aux seuils sans fleurs sans mains tendues,
quelque part dans le lieu des vérités ardues
vous m'avez parlé bas de choses convenues,
d'un ciel sans ornement, de routes absolues
et d'un renoncement total à l'étendue.
(La mort dans la muraille anonyme remue.)

XV

Une route se remémore
tous les pas disparus.
Mais elle attend et rien encore
n'est vraiment apparu.

XVI

Sous un vague sourire
sourdement tu t'opposes.
Sous ce portrait de cire
tu parles d'autre chose.

Le nuage ivre d'eau
n'est pas aussi menteur!
Recouvert de douleur,
tu ris, tu chantes faux.

En vain tu t'évertues:
nul ne s'y laisse prendre.

XVII

À la mâchoire serrée
sur un trop brûlant secret
les paroles préférées
se proposent sans arrêt.

XIV

Outskirt virtue, strictness of streets
ever unruffled by nebulous forms,
empty between your rails, serious, circumspect,
no doorstep smiles, no flowers, no proffered hands,
somewhere in the abode of ardent truths,
you have softly spoken of things agreed,
of unadorned heavens, of absolute paths
and complete renunciation of space.
(Death stirs in the anonymous wall.)

XV

A road again calls to mind
All the steps disappeared.
But waits and nothing still
has really appeared.

XVI

Beneath a vague smile
your deafness resists.
Waxen-faced while
the subject desists.

The cloud drunk on water
is no more untrue!
Blanketed in sorrow,
you laugh out of key.

Try as you might,
no one is fooled.

XVII

To the jaw clenched firm
on a secret too sensitive
favourite words
are constantly proffered.

La poitrine se soulève.
Frappez, souffles furieux!
Tout retient, mais rien n'achève
l'ouragan silencieux.

Rien ne bouge que les cieux,
rien ne brille que les yeux.

XVIII

Encore une commotion!
J'avance avec la vie.
Les portes tremblent comme font
les feuilles sous la pluie.

Que de secousses dans le cœur
le sang et la pensée!
Encore un pas vers la splendeur
des formes dépassées!

Terre profonde comme l'eau,
de lumières mêlée
ce qui est là vient de si haut,
que d'étoiles tombées!

Tout ce que vous m'avez appris
s'est chargé de souffrance,
tout ce que vous m'avez repris
s'est comblé de silence.

Le vin de mon âme, le vin
dans mes membres bouillonne.
O jours! serait-ce donc en vain
que vos routes résonnent?

The breast is bursting.
Beat and blow, frantic breath!
All holds back and nothing completes
the silent hurricane.

Nothing moves but the heavens,
nothing shines but the eyes.

XVIII

Another excitement!
I move forward with life.
Doors quiver just
like leaves in the rain.

How many tremors in the heart
in the blood and in thought!
One more step towards the splendour
of forms long past!

Earth deep as water
and mingled with lights
what is there comes from so high,
how many fallen stars!

All that you have taught me
is burdened with suffering,
all that you have taken back
has filled itself with silence.

Wine of my soul, wine
fomenting in my limbs.
Days! Is it thus in vain
that your roads resound?

La seine de Paris

De ceux qui préférant à leurs regrets les fleuves
et à leurs souvenirs les profonds monuments
aiment l'eau qui descend au partage des villes,
la Seine de Paris me sait le plus fidèle
à ses quais adoucis de livres. Pas un souffle
qui ne vienne vaincu par les mains des remous
sans me trouver prêt à le prendre et à relire
dans ses cheveux le chant des montagnes, pas un
silence dans les nuits d'été où je ne glisse
comme une feuille entre l'air et le flot, pas une aile
blanche d'oiseau remontant de la mer
ne longe le soleil sans m'arracher d'un cri
strident à ma pesanteur monotone! Les piliers
sont lourds après le pas inutile et je plonge
par eux jusqu'à la terre et quand
je remonte et ruisselle et m'ébroue,
j'invoque un dieu qui regarde aux fenêtres
et brille de plaisir dans les vitres caché.
Protégé par ses feux je lutte de vitesse
en moi-même avec l'eau qui ne veut pas attendre
et du fardeau des bruits de pas et de voitures
et de marteaux sur des tringles et de voix
tant de rapidité me délivre…Les quais
et les tours sont déjà loin lorsque soudain
je les retrouve, recouvrant comme les siècles,
avec autant d'amour et de terreur, vague après vague,
méandres de l'esprit la courbe de mon fleuve.

The Seine in Paris

Since I prefer rivers to regrets
the grave profundity of monuments to memories,
love the water's flow dividing cities,
the Seine in Paris knows me deeply faithful
to its gentle book-lined quays. Not a breath
arrives defeated by the eddying waters
but that I am ready to take it and to read again
in its hair the mountain song, not a
summer night-time silence but that I glide
like a leaf between air and water, not a white
gull's wing returned from the sea pursuing the sun
but that I am wrenched from the weight of my monotony
by a strident cry! The pillars weigh heavy
after the unnecessary step and I plunge
by them to earth, and when I climb up again
streaming and shake myself,
I invoke a god who looks through windows
and gleams with pleasure in the panes.
Protected by his rays I conduct an inner race
with water which will not wait
and from the burden of footsteps and motorcar noises
the beating of hammers on bars and voices
that rapid flow frees me...Quaysides
and towers are already far away when
suddenly I rediscover them
covering like the centuries
with equal love and equal terror, wave upon wave,
meanderings of the mind and the bend of my river.

FIGURES
FIGURES
(1944)

Cézanne

Comme au-dessus du ciel il y a le ciel et après la vie la vie, – au-delà du regard il y a le regard.

Apre, violent, obstiné, le regard qui jaillit comme l'étincelle entre deux pierres, – et sa joie confine à la panique et son élan si loin l'engage qu'il menace à la fois le secret de l'esprit et celui des choses.

Lieu caché au fond du plein jour, domaine du feu primitif et des surprises de la condensation, second regard! C'est là qu'au milieu du strident silence des cigales, un Enchanteur seul, fumant de colère et de volonté, fait effort pour rapprocher peu à peu l'une de l'autre les rebelles et rivales évidences du monde sensible et de la pensée impalpable.

Tandis que d'autres cherchent la lumière (cette abstraction), il écarte d'un geste le poudroiement des rayons et, possédé par les fureurs de la découverte, il touche à la nature des choses: la Couleur.

Une parure? – Non! Un masque? – Non! l'Être même! Vérité venue du centre des objets, puisée à leur substance, lentement repoussée sur leurs bords par le travail des intimes échanges, purifiée par son ascension, hissée enfin à son comble: l'air libre, – plus elle s'évapore, plus elle se renouvelle et plus elle reste fraîche aux lèvres des yeux altérés.

Oui. Fraîche. Acide. Verte. Minérale. Absolue. Couleur, pierre de la construction du monde, degré d'intensité des formes (qu'elle étire et modèle à son gré), limite et lien des éléments, inséparable de la Création, comme elle inépuisable…

Telle dans sa splendeur elle est donc aussi le secret, le carrefour magique et mouvant où se rencontrent l'âme qui voit et les présences qui sont vues. Sans quitter les plans qu'elle a construits, elle se plaît aux métamorphoses, s'altère quand tournent les volumes, quand les spectacles s'éloignent. Elle se meut dans son propre mystère et fait bouger plus loin qu'elles-mêmes, dans le sillage des planètes, ailleurs, là-bas où nous ne sommes pas encore, les éclatantes et souveraines masses d'une pomme, d'une chaise, d'un rideau d'arbres ou des joueurs de cartes soudain figés dans leur mouvement personnel par l'élan de la bourrasque invisible qui les entraîne.

Désormais sûre d'elle-même, cette puissance enfin peut se permettre les plus délicats des jeux: sur la feuille transparente de

Cézanne

Just as beyond the sky is the sky, beyond life, life, – beyond seeing is seeing.

Harsh, violent, stubborn, that moment of seeing which flashes like a spark between two flints – and the joy it induces touches on panic, and its irruption involves it so far that it threatens the secret of the mind and the secret of things.

A private space hidden in the full light of day, realm of primitive fire and the surprises of condensation, second act of seeing! There, in the strident silence of grasshoppers, a solitary Enchanter, fuming with rage and with will power, struggles gradually to bring together the rebellious and rival affirmations of the sensible world and impalpable thought.

Where others seek light (that abstraction), he brushes aside at a stroke the shimmering of rays, and, possessed by the fury of discovery, touches on the nature of things: Colour.

A raiment? – No! A mask? – No! Being itself! Truth deriving from the core of objects, drawn from the well of their substance, slowly displaced towards their edges by the working of intimate exchanges, purified by its ascension, finally drawn up to its pinnacle: free air, – the more it evaporates, the more it is renewed, the more it retains its coolness on the lips of quenched eyes.

Yes. Cool. Sharp. Green. Mineral. Absolute. Colour, the world's keystone, point of intensity of forms (which it draws out and models at its will), limit and link of the elements, inseparable from Creation, and like Creation, inexhaustible...

Such in its splendour is it also the secret, the magic and moving intersection of the seeing soul and seen presences. Without leaving the planes it has constructed, it takes pleasure in metamorphoses, changes as volumes turn, as spectacles recede. Its movement takes place within its own mystery, and gives movement elsewhere, in regions we have not yet attained, in the wake of the planets, beyond themselves, to the shattering sovereign masses of an apple, a chair, a curtain of trees or a group of card-players, suddenly frozen in their own movement by the surge of the invisible squall which carries them on.

Confident now, this force can finally allow itself the most exquisite form of play: on the transparent leaf of the stretched surface, a few light touches, a handful of hints, sometimes suffice to build a mountain.

l'étendue, parfois quelques touches légères, une poignée d'allusions suffisent à bâtir une montagne.

Alors, entre les teintes espacées, il n'y a plus que des lacunes sans visage, il n'y a plus que le vide. Pourtant on voit que la montagne tient toujours.

C'est comme si (je tremble de le dire), comme si peu à peu la réalité se mélangeait à une sorte d'absence toute-puissante...

Et tout à coup notre cœur s'arrête. L'Enchanteur a trouvé: terre, mer et ciel, le monde vient de basculer dans l'esprit.

Then, in the spaces between the touches of colour, there are no more than faceless gaps, no more than the void. And yet, manifestly, the mountain still stands.

As though (I tremble to say it), as though gradually reality were mingling with a kind of omnipotent absence...

And suddenly our heart misses its beat: the Enchanter has won his trick: earth, sea and sky, the world has been thrown off its axis in the mind.

À l'octroi du point-du-jour

Henri Rousseau le douanier
(à Marcel Arland)

C'est le commencement, le monde est à repeindre,
l'herbe veut être verte, elle a besoin de nos regards;
les maisons où l'on vit, les routes où l'on marche,
les jardins, les bateaux, les barrières
m'attendent pour entrer dans leur vrai paradis.
Je ne suis pas ici pour me moquer des choses;
dans mes yeux qui les recueillent elles font de beaux rêves
et dans mes yeux puis dans mes mains elles deviennent sages,
égales et polies comme des images.
Je voudrais être du ciel l'absolu photographe
et pour l'éternité fixer la noce de Juillet,
la mariée comme une crème et la grand-mère qui se tasse
et le caniche noir et les invités à moustache
qui sont de la même famille.

J'empêcherais pour toujours de bouger
les voiles blanches qui vont sur l'Oise,
les branches aux feuilles nombreuses
des chênes, des peupliers et surtout des acacias
et les nuages montagneux et l'eau de la Seine
pour qu'elle devienne lisse comme un canal.

J'empêcherais aussi de s'en aller de la mémoire
les souvenirs de notre service militaire
dans les pays épais des Colonies
et côte à côte rassemblés comme par un songe
je placerais sur les étagères du monde,
avec leurs couleurs véritables et devenues sans danger,
la charrette du voisin et son cheval tout neuf
dans l'avenue de banlieue aux arbres ronds
et les flamants et les grands lotus et les petits palmiers,
le gros enfant apoplectique et son pantin
et le tigre méchant et ma femme défunte
et les singes suceurs de gros soleils orange.

Dawn's Customs Point
Douanier Rousseau
(to Marcel Arland)

It is the beginning, the world needs repainting,
the grass wishes to be green, requires our gaze;
the houses we live in, the roads we walk,
the gardens, the boats, the gates
are waiting for me to enter their true paradise.
I am not here to laugh at things,
in my enveloping eyes they dream beautiful dreams
and in my eyes and then in my hands they become good,
and even and smooth as images.
I should like to become the absolute photographer of the sky
eternally fix the nuptials of July,
the bride like a cream-cake and the shrunken grandmother
and the black poodle and the mustachioed guests
who are all of the same family.

I would freeze for ever the movement
of the white sails on the river Oise,
the many-leaved branches
of the oak trees, the poplars, and particularly the acacias
and the mountainous clouds and the waters of the Seine
which I would make smooth and flat as a canal.

I would also freeze in the memory
recollections of National Service in dense Colonial countries
and collected side by side as in a dream
I would place on the shelves of the world
in their true colours divested of danger
the neighbour's cart and his brand-new horse
in the suburban avenue with its round trees
and the flamingoes and the huge lotuses and the tiny palm trees
the fat apoplectic child and its puppet
and the wicked tiger and my departed wife
and the monkeys sucking enormous orange suns.

Et moi-même en veston la palette à la main
aux portes de l'octroi sous les drapeaux du jour,
devant le pont où je vois tous les réverbères
et les maisons dont j'ai bien séparé les cheminées
afin que le vent tourne autour d'elles,
je resterais debout très grand dans le ciel départemental,
j'arrêterais pour vous les heures d'aujourd'hui.

And I myself, jacketed, palette in hand
at the customs gates under daylight's flags
in front of the bridge where I see all the lamps
and the houses whose chimneys
I have carefully separated
so that the wind can turn around them,
shall stand there tall in the Departmental sky;
I shall freeze for you this day's hours.

PETRIFIED DAYS
JOURS PÉTRIFIÉS
(1947)

Sommeil sans fin

Silence autour du tonnerre
moribond par un brasier
secrètement habité
prolongé et dévoré
je dormais près de la terre,
je dormais je dors encore
très longtemps je dormirai
replié sur la torture
sur les monstres familiers
dont je suis l'aliment.

Voici le jour, perfide
parure de mon néant!
Mon sommeil change de face.
L'eternité que je porte
est bornée de toutes parts;
sur les ombres de Paris
les plumes de la lumière
anges gardiens de ma nuit
ont leur grave sourire:
«Tu n'iras pas plus avant!»
Mais que m'importent ces vitres
brisées, inutiles
par où tombe tout le ciel!
Dans les cavernes du sang
dans mes puits où se regarde
l'espace multiplié
pas à pas je descends.

Foudre rayons météores
dons de l'irréalité
le possible l'impossible
la profonde liberté,
votre feu brûle mes veines,
je frissonne sans bouger.
Près de la terre où je dors
votre cristal m'illumine,
vos traits sont mes ossements
ma vie et ma mort.

Endless Sleep

Silence surrounds the death-thrown
thunder secretly inhabited
extended and devoured
by living embers
Close to the earth I slept,
slept on and still sleep on
long shall I still sleep on
falling back upon the torture
upon the domestic monsters
which I nourish.

Here comes the traitor dawn
adornment of my void.
My slumber turns the other face.
The eternity I bear within me
is circumscribed on every side;
the plumes of light
guardian angels of my night
cast their solemn smile
over the Paris darkness:
'No further shall you go!'
But what are to me those shattered
pointless panes
through which the whole sky falls!
Step by step I make my way
down into the caves of blood
down into the darkness of my pits
where space multiplied
contemplates itself.

Lightning rays meteors
gifts of unreality
what might be and what cannot be
depths of freedom,
your fire burns in my veins
and motionless I shiver.
Close to the earth where I sleep
your crystal is my illumination,
your features are my whitened bones
my life and my death.

C

Incarnation
(à André Frénaud)

Un être grave douloureux
qui vient du fond des âges
un être lourd et malheureux
remonte jusqu'à mon visage,
emprunte ma voix pour parler,
pour se parer d'une personne
qui prenne jour sur l'autre bord.
La bouche et les yeux qu'il se donne
encore obscurcis par la mort
affleurent aux vivantes rives:
ah choc profond de la clarté!
la lumière circule et danse
les sons s'enroulent aux oreilles
flux et reflux surabondance
bouleversé par l'évidence
il va de merveille en merveille
dans les gorges de la santé.
O nourriture pour cet ogre
qui n'était encor que gosier
sans nom sans forme, rien que gouffre –
bon pour la nuit et la fumée:
voici que telle chose existe
qui dans la main pèse et persiste
voici la pierre de nos dieux
les colonnes au long des routes
les portes battant sous les voûtes
et les arbres infranchissables.
Il dit: parle! – et j'ouvre la bouche
et les vieux échos enroués
par ma colère secoués
tonnent sur le tambour des murs;
il dit: marche! – et mon pas l'emporte
plus sonore qu'une cohorte
comme ce peuple de portraits
que dans le jeu profond des glaces
enfante un couple de reflets.
Je suis le fils je suis le père
de ce multiple interminable;

Incarnation
(to André Frénaud)

A solemn and mournful being
come from the very depths of time
a weighty and weary being
rises within me to my face,
borrows my voice for utterance,
to deck itself in human form
and emerge on the other side.
The mouth and eyes which it assumes
still overshadowed now by death
brush the edge of the living shores:
Ah, the sudden shock of clarity!
light and shadow weave and dance
sounds wind themselves around the ears
ebb and flow and overflow
overwhelmed by evidence
it moves from miracle to miracle
in the deepest gorges of health.
Food for this ravenous ogre
which was yet no more than gullet
nameless and formless, no more than gulf –
fit only for night and for smoke:
so it is that such a thing exists
weighs in the hand and persists
thus the stone of our gods
the columns lining the roads
the doors swinging beneath the vaults
and the impassable trees.
Speak! it says – I open my mouth
and the old rasping echoes
shaken by my anger
thunder against the drumskin walls;
Walk! it says – and away we go
with more clatter than a cohort
like those populous portraits
spawned by a pair of reflections
in the profound play of mirrors.
I am the son I am the father
of this interminable multitude;

lui donnant corps je le mélange
à l'eau à la terre et au vent
je suis la gueule du volcan
pour cette vapeur inconnue
montant des profondeurs du monde
à la surface de nos champs.
Je déchaîne dans le visible
l'appétit de sa cécité,
je délivre dans l'air des formes
sa dévorante opacité
et dans l'instant faible et léger
l'immémoriale impatience
qu'il a de se manifester...
Mais malheur à lui s'il retrouve,
en levant les yeux par mes yeux
plus haut que la tendre lumière
plus loin que le ciel habité,
les ténèbres qu'il voulait fuir,
l'inconsistance qu'il abhorre
et les fumées qui l'épouvantent
menaçant la vie et la mort!

                *

Il dit:
        «Vous songerez à moi
vous qui vivez,
quand je fondrai dans l'empyrée
comme une haleine!
Mes feux par vous auront passé
vous laissant alourdis de peur
de faim de guerre et d'incendie,
honteux du souvenir des fleurs
honteux de risquer un regard
sur le corsage de vos femmes.
J'aurai coulé dans votre sang
j'aurai troqué l'inexistence
qui m'habillait de ses brouillards
contre un instant près des rochers
des os des métaux et des dents,
contre un bras qui se lève et hèle

lending it body I mingle it
with water earth and wind
I am the gaping volcano's mouth
for this unknown vapour
rising from the depths of the world
to the surface of our fields.
I unleash into the visible
the appetite for its blindness,
release into the air of forms
its devouring opacity
and into the slight and slender instant
its immemorial impatient
desire to manifest itself...
But woe betide it if it rediscovers,
lifting its eyes through my eyes
higher than the gentle light
further than the inhabited heavens,
the shadows which it sought to flee,
the inconsistency it hates
the smoke which horrifies it
threatening both life and death!

                    *

It says:
            'You will think of me
you who live,
when I melt like a breath
in celestial fire!
Through you my flames will have passed
leaving you weighed down with fear
with hunger with war and with fire
ashamed of memories of flowers
ashamed to chance a fleeting glance
at your women's breasts.
I shall have seeped into your blood
bartered the non-existence
which clothed me in its mists
against a moment near the rocks
the bones the metals and the teeth
against a raised and hailing arm

contre un baiser aux infidèles
contre le pas, contre le poing!
Mais pour avoir ainsi calmé
ma soif de monter dans l'aurore
vous serez bien récompensés!
Tandis que pleurant vos visages
(même écrasés sur vos tombeaux)
je repleuvrai sur vos hameaux
sous forme de cendre et d'orage
forçant vos piètres horizons
brisant les tuiles de vos toits
crevant la panse de vos coffres
j'aurai glissé dans votre bouche
le goût d'une absence infinie,
j'aurai laissé l'eau dans vos caves,
la flamme au bord de vos maisons,
l'abîme au bout de vos chemins,
le doute au fond de vos pensées
et le tremblement dans vos mains!»

*

Comment comment, puisque c'est moi,
bâillonner cette bouche affreuse?
Elle dit bien ce que nous sommes,
un moment déguisés en hommes
avant d'éclater par la nuit
qui gonfle nos frêles parois.
Mais quel orgueil de se connaître
effacés avant d'apparaître!
Quel rire secret sur nos dents!
Quel honneur dans le moindre instant!
Quel phosphore sur nos charniers,
quel feu plus long que nos bûchers,
éblouit nos pires ténèbres
et quelle perle au fond du temps!
S'il n'est plus rien qui soit demain,
quelle injure aux mille complices
du grand fantôme souterrain,
à travers mensonge et supplices,
que s'efforcer vers l'être humain
pendant le bref éclair du jour.

against kissing the unfaithful
against a step against a fist!
But for having thus appeased
my thirst for rising into the dawn
you will find ample recompense!
While mourning your faces
(even crushed on your tombs)
I shall rain again on your hamlets
in the form of ashes and storm
forcing your meagre horizons
smashing the tiles on your roofs
stoving in your coffers
I shall have slipped into your mouth
the taste of an infinite absence,
I shall have left water in your cellars
flames at the edge of your houses
the abyss at the end of your ways
doubt in the depths of your thoughts
and trembling in your hands!'

                    *

How, how, since it is myself
can I gag this hideous mouth?
It speaks truly what we are,
for a moment disguised as men
before bursting with the night
which swells our fragile skin.
But what pride in self-knowledge
erasure preceding appearance.
What secret laughter grits our teeth!
What honour in the slightest moment!
What phosphorus on our charnel houses,
what fire slower than our martyr's stake
lightens our deepest darkness
and what a pearl in the depths of time!
If nothing is which tomorrow will be
what affront to the myriad accomplices
of the great subterranean phantom,
through torture and through lies
to struggle towards humanity
in daylight's brief flashes.

Ombre cette ombre monstrueuse
qui vient du fond des âges,
cette ombre grave et malheureuse
remontée jusqu'à nos visages,
nous la traînerons elle-même
comme au soleil une fumée
jusque sous l'arche de l'amour.

Shade that monstrous shade
which comes from the depths of time,
that sombre serious shade
which rises to our faces
we shall drag it
to the very arch of love
like smoke in the sun.

MISTER SIR
MONSIEUR MONSIEUR
(1951)

Monsieur Monsieur
(1948-1950)

Argument

C'est au carrefour de Burlesque et du Lyrique (il faisait froid, le vent de l'espace agitait les haillons d'un épouvantail), c'est sur ce miteux théâtre de marionnettes où vont tout à l'heure apparaître deux Monsieurs identiques dont chacun n'est que l'ombre de l'autre, des jocrisses jouant au philosophe, des éléments éternels réduits à des dimensions ridicules, des sentiments vrais représentés par leur propre parodie, – c'est là que je m'étais caché pour écrire ces poèmes.

On trouvera donc ici presque plus de pantomimes et de grimaces que de mots. Si le lecteur consent à devenir complice du jeu, s'il parle et vit mes fantoches en les lisant, s'il entend sa propre voix intérieure moduler des accents grotesques, irréels à force de niaiserie, s'il sent son masque parcouru de tics nerveux, annonciateurs d'une gesticulation idiote et libératrice, –
alors

MONSIEUR MONSIEUR

aura gagné.

I. *Monsieur interroge Monsieur*

Monsieur, pardonnez-moi
de vous importuner:
quel bizarre chapeau
vous avez sur la tête!

– Monsieur vous vous trompez
car je n'ai plus de tête
comment voulez-vous donc
que je porte un chapeau!

Mister Sir
(1948-1950)

Argument

The action takes place at the intersection between the Lyric and
the Burlesque (it was cold and the scarecrow's rags were flapping in
the winds of space), here on this flea-pit puppet theatre there will
shortly appear two identical gentlemen, each of whom is but the
shadow of the other, ham actors playing at philosophy, elements of
eternity reduced to the proportions of the absurd, truth and
sincerity acted out by parodies of themselves – here it was I hid to
write these poems.

So here you will find mime and grimace rather than words. If the
reader is prepared to enter into the game, if he can live and speak
my puppets as he reads them, if he can hear his own inner voice
intone grotesque inflections, unreal by their idiocy, if he can feel his
own mask infected with a nervous twitch, vaunt-courier of
ridiculous and liberating gesticulations, –
then
MISTER SIR

will have won.

I. *Mister questions Sir*

Sir, I'm so terribly sorry
to bother you:
what a strange hat
you have on your head!

– Sir, you are mistaken
for I have lost my head
so how on earth
can I wear a hat!

– Et quel est cet habit
dont vous êtes vêtu?

– Monsieur je le regrette
mais je n'ai plus de corps
et n'ayant plus de corps
je ne mets plus d'habit.

– Pourtant lorsque je parle
Monsieur vous répondez
et cela m'encourage
à vous interroger:
Monsieur quels sont ces gens
que je vois rassemblés
et qui semblent attendre
avant de s'avancer?

– Monsieur ce sont des arbres
dans une plaine immense,
ils ne peuvent bouger
car ils sont attachés.

– Monsieur Monsieur Monsieur
au-dessus de nos têtes
quels sont ces yeux nombreux
qui dans la nuit regardent?

– Monsieur ce sont des astres
ils tournent sur eux-mêmes
et ne regardent rien.

– Monsieur quels sont ces cris
quelque part on dirait
on dirait que l'on rit
on dirait que l'on pleure
on dirait que l'on souffre?

– Monsieur ce sont les dents
les dents de l'océan
qui mordent les rochers
sans avoir soif ni faim
et sans férocité.

– And what is that coat
you wear upon your back?

– Sir, I'm terribly sorry
but I have lost my body
and no longer have a back
on which to wear a coat.

And yet when I speak Sir
you seem to reply
which gives me encouragement
in still asking you questions:
Sir who are those people
I see gathered there
and who seem to be waiting
before going on?

– Sir those are trees
in a measureless plain,
they cannot move for
they are bound to the earth.

– Sir Mister Sir
there above our heads
what are those numerous eyes
looking out into the night?

– Sir they are stars
they turn upon themselves
they look out on nothing.

– Sir what are those cries
in a way you might think
you might think you heard laughter
you might think you heard tears
you might think you heard suffering?

Sir those are the teeth
the ocean's teeth
biting the rocks
without hunger or thirst
without anger as well.

– Monsieur quels sont ces actes
ces mouvements de feux
ces déplacements d'air
ces déplacements d'astres
roulements de tambour
roulements de tonnerre
on dirait des armées
qui partent pour la guerre
sans avoir d'ennemi?

– Monsieur c'est la matière
qui s'enfante elle-même
et se fait des enfants
pour se faire la guerre.

– Monsieur soudain ceci
soudain ceci m'étonne
il n'y a plus personne
pourtant moi je vous parle
et vous, vous m'entendez
puisque vous répondez!

– Monsieur ce sont les choses
qui ne voient ni entendent
mais qui voudraient entendre
et qui voudraient parler.

– Monsieur à travers tout
quelles sont ces images
tantôt en liberté
et tantôt enfermées
cette énorme pensée
où des figures passent
où brillent des couleurs?

– Monsieur c'était l'espace
et l'espace
se meurt.

– Sir what are those actions
those fires forming fours
those movements of air
those displacements of stars
those rolls of drums and thunder
you might think you heard armies
preparing for war
with no one to fight?

– Sir that is matter
giving birth to itself
bringing forth infants
to make war on itself

– Sir all this suddenly
suddenly leaves me surprised
there is no one left
and yet I address you
and you seem to be hearing me
since you reply!

– Sir those are the things
that neither see nor hear
but which long to hear
and long to speak

– Sir throughout all this
what are those images
sometimes imprisoned
and sometimes free
that measureless thought
in which figures pass
and colours glow?

– Sir that was space
and space
gives up the ghost.

II. *Voyage avec Monsieur Monsieur*

Avec Monsieur Monsieur
je m'en vais en voyage.
Bien qu'ils n'existent pas
je porte leurs bagages.
Je suis seul ils sont deux.

Lorsque le train démarre
je vois sur leur visage
la satisfaction
de rester immobiles
quand tout fuit autour d'eux.

Comme ils sont face à face
chacun a ses raisons.
L'un dit: les choses viennent
et l'autre: elles s'en vont.

Quand le train les dépasse
est-ce que les maisons
subsistent ou s'effacent?
moi je dis qu'après nous
ne reste rien du tout.

– Voyez comme vous êtes!
lui répond le premier,
pour vous rien ne s'arrête
moi je vois l'horizon
de champs et de villages
longuement persister.
Nous sommes le passage
nous sommes la fumée...

C'est ainsi qu'ils devisent
et la discussion
devient si difficile
qu'ils perdent la raison.

Alors le train s'arrête
avec le paysage
alors tout se confond.

II. *Journey with Mister Sir*

With Mister Sir
I set out to travel.
Although they don't exist
I carry their bags.
I am alone and they are two.

When the train draws out
I read upon their faces
the satisfaction
of remaining stationary
while everyone around them flees.

As they are face to face
each thinks his own thoughts.
One says: things come
the other says: things go.

As the train passes
do the houses
stay or go?
I say that when we go
nothing stays at all.

– See the way you are!
replies one,
for you nothing stops
whereas I see the horizon
made up of fields and villages
going on for ever.
We are passing
we are smoke...

And so they go on
and the conversation
becomes so difficult
they lose their senses.

So the train stops
and the landscape too
and all gets muddled up.

III. *Monsieur Monsieur aux bains de mer*

Un jour près de la mer
Monsieur et Monsieur seuls
parlaient tranquillement
et mangeaient une pomme
en regardant les cieux.

— Voyez donc, dit l'un d'eux,
l'agréable néant!
et quel apaisement
quand l'abîme sans bord
mélange sans effort
les choses et les gens!
Pour qui ressemble à Dieu
les jours particuliers
ne sont pas nécessaires.

— La question n'est pas là
Monsieur (répond Monsieur)
nous sommes éphémères,
or la totalité
de la grande Unité
nous étant refusée,
c'est par la quantité
que nous nous en tirons.
Et nous additionnons
et nous thésaurisons!
Donc la diversité
pour nous sur cette terre
est la nécessité.
Regardez ce poisson
qui n'est pas un oiseau
qui n'est pas une pomme
qui n'est pas la baleine
qui n'est pas le bateau...

— Ah, pour moi c'est tout comme,
interrompit Monsieur,
la baleine et la pomme
devant l'éternité
sont à égalité.

III. *Mister Sir at the Seaside*

One day by the seaside
Mister and Sir sat together
talking quietly amongst themselves
eating an apple
and looking up at the heavens.

– Regard, said one,
the comfort of the void!
and the peace that ensues
when the measureless abyss
effortlessly mingles
people and things!
For those in God's image
particular days
have no necessity.

That is not the question
Sir (replies Mister)
we all are ephemeral
and given that we are refused
the totality of Unity
we have to get by
on quantity.
So we add it all up
pile coin on coin.
And thus diversity
here on this earth for us
is the only necessity.
Look at that fish
it's not a bird
it's not an apple
it's not a whale
it's not a boat...

– Might as well be for me,
interjects Mister,
in face of eternity
between the whale and the apple
equality rules.

A ces mots le vent souffle
emportant leurs chapeaux
et les deux personnages
dans le ciel bleu et beau
s'effacent aussitôt.

IV. *Les difficultés essentielles*

Monsieur met ses chaussettes
Monsieur les lui retire.

Monsieur met sa culotte
Monsieur la lui déchire.

Monsieur met sa chemise
Monsieur met ses bretelles
Monsieur met son veston
Monsieur met ses chaussures:
au fur et à mesure
Monsieur les fait valser.

Quand Monsieur se promène
Monsieur reste au logis

quand Monsieur est ici
Monsieur n'est jamais là

quand Monsieur fait l'amour
Monsieur fait pénitence

s'il prononce un discours
il garde le silence,

s'il part pour la forêt
c'est qu'il s'installe en ville,

lorsqu'il reste tranquille
c'est qu'il est inquiet

At these words the wind comes up
and blows away their hats
and the two figures
evaporate
into the clear blue sky.

IV. *Essential Difficulties*

Mister puts on his socks
Sir takes them off.

Sir puts on his underpants
Mister rips them off.

Mister puts on his shirt
Sir puts on his braces
Mister puts on his jacket
Sir puts on his shoes
while
Mister gets them on the trot.

When Sir takes a walk
Mister remains in residence

when Mister is here
Sir is never there

when Sir makes love
Mister does penance

if he makes a speech
he keeps his peace,

if he goes out in the woods
he's setting himself up in town,

when he keeps his peace
it's because he's not calm

il dort quand il s'éveille
il pleure quand il rit

au lever du soleil
voici venir la nuit;

Vrai! c'est vertigineux
de le voir coup sur coup
tantôt seul tantôt deux
levé couché levé
debout assis debout!

Il ôte son chapeau
il remet son chapeau
chapeau pas de chapeau
pas de chapeau chapeau
et jamais de repos.

V. *Le tombeau de Monsieur Monsieur*

Dans un silence épais
Monsieur et Monsieur parlent
c'est comme si Personne
avec Rien dialoguait.

L'un dit: Quand vient la mort
pour chacun d'entre nous
c'est comme si personne
'avait jamais été.
Aussitôt disparu
qui vous dit que je fus?

– Monsieur, repond Monsieur,
plus loin que vous j'irai:
aujourd'hui ou jamais
je ne sais si j'étais.
Le temps marche si vite
qu'au moment où je parle
(indicatif-présent)
je ne suis déjà plus
ce que j'étais avant.

he sleeps when he wakes
he weeps when he laughs

at the rising of the sun
there comes the evening twilight;

True, it's enough to make you dizzy
to see him time and time again
sometimes one and sometimes two
up and down and down and up
standing sitting standing!

He takes off his hat
and puts on his hat
hat's on hat's off
hat's off hat's on
and never a moment's peace.

V. *Memorial to Mister Sir*

In a heavy silence
Mister and Sir are talking
as though No one
were conversing with Nothing.

Says one: When death comes
for each of us
it is as though no one
had ever been.
Once I'm gone
who could say I was?

– Sir, replies Mister,
further than you I'll go:
today or ever
I know not whether I used to be.
Time marches on so fast
that at the moment of speaking
(present indicative)
I am no longer
what I was before.

Si je parle au passé
ce n'est pas même assez
il faudrait je le sens
l'indicatif-néant.

– C'est vrai, reprend Monsieur,
sur ce mode inconnu
je conterai ma vie
notre vie à tous deux:
À nous les souvenirs!
Nous ne sommes pas nés
nous n'avons pas grandi
nous n'avons pas rêvé
nous n'avons pas dormi
nous n'avons pas mangé
nous n'avons pas aimé.

Nous ne sommes personne
et rien n'est arrivé.

To speak in the past
is still not sufficient
what I might need I feel
is the indicative of the void.

– True enough, replies Mister,
in this unknown mood
I shall recount my life
our life together:
Here's to nostalgia!
We were not born
we did not grow up
we did not dream
we did not sleep
we did not eat
we did not love.

We are no one
and nothing ever happened.

À mots couverts
(Sur le ton de la basse médisance.)

Savez-vous la nouvelle?
               – Ma foi non!
                           – Il paraît…
(mais soyez courageux, attendez-vous au pire!)
il paraît que le Temps par une nuit sans lune…
vous devinez?
          – Hélas, je n'ai que trop compris,
ô Dieux, est-ce possible?
               – Telle est la vérité!
– Quoi, dites-vous, le Temps et la Nuit?…
                               – Elle-même!
– C'était donc pour cela que ces deux misérables!
J'aurais dû m'en douter!
               – Ce serait beaucoup dire:
tout s'est passé sans bruit
comme un léger frisson pendant un long sommeil.
– Et nous les orphelins, qu'allons-nous devenir?

La nuit le silence et l'au-delà

Un soupir dans l'espace énorme

Puis une voix murmure:

          «Gontran, es-tu là?»

Pas de réponse

Des pas s'en vont comme les nuages.

92

A Nod's as Good as a Wink
(In a tone of malicious gossip.)

Have you heard the news?
                    – Heavens, no!
                                        – They say...
(just be brave, prepare to hear the worst!)
they say that Time on a dark and moonless night...
can you guess?
                    – Alas, too well I comprehend,
ye gods, but can this be?
                    – The truth will out!
– What, say you? Time and Night?...
                                        – The very same!
– That is why those miserable wretches!
I should have guessed!
                    – That would be saying a lot:
it was very discreet
like a gentle tremor in the midst of slumber.
– And we poor orphans, what shall we become?

Night Silence and the Beyond

A sigh in the enormity of space

And then a murmur:

        'Gontran, are you there?'

No reply

Footsteps disappearing like clouds.

Conversation
(Sur le pas de la porte, avec bonhomie.)

Comment ça va sur la terre?
– Ça va ça va, ça va bien.

Les petits chiens sont-ils prospères?
– Mon Dieu oui merci bien.

Et les nuages?
– Ça flotte.

Et les volcans?
– Ça mijote.

Et les fleuves?
– Ça s'écoule.

Et le temps?
– Ça se déroule.

Et votre âme?
– Elle est malade
le printemps était trop vert
elle a mangé trop de salade.

La môme néant
(Voix de marionnette, voix de fausset, aiguë,
nasillarde, cassée, cassante, caquetante, édentée.)

Quoi qu'a dit?
– A dit rin.

Quoi qu'a fait?
– A fait rin.

A quoi qu'a pense?
– A pense à rin.

Chat

(On the doorstep, hail fellow well met.)

How's things on earth?
– All right, not so bad, pretty good in fact.

The little dogs doing all right?
– Yes, thank the Lord.

And the clouds?
– Heavenly.

And the volcanoes?
– On the boil.

And the rivers?
– Running smoothly.

And time?
– Passing fair.

And your soul?
– A little poorly
Spring too green
bolted its lettuce.

Ragamuffin Nuffin'

*(Puppet's voice, falsetto, nasal, sharp,
brittle, cracked, cackling, toothless.)*

What d's'e say?
– Don't say nuffink.

What d's'e do?
– Don't do nuffink

What d's'e fink?
– Don't fink nuffink.

Pourquoi qu'a dit rin?
Pourquoi qu'a fait rin?
Pourquoi qu'a pense à rin?

– A'xiste pas.

Conseils donnés par une sorcière
(À voix basse, avec un air épouvanté,
à l'oreille du lecteur.)

Retenez-vous de rire
dans le petit matin!

N'écoutez pas les arbres
qui gardent les chemins!

Ne dites votre nom
à la terre endormie
qu'après minuit sonné!

À la neige, à la pluie
ne tendez pas la main!

N'ouvrez votre fenêtre
qu'aux petites planètes
que vous connaissez bien!

Confidence pour confidence:
vous qui venez me consulter,
méfiance, méfiance!
On ne sait pas ce qui peut arriver.

Why d's'e say nuffink?
Why d's'e do nuffink?
Why d's'e fink nuffink?

– Ain't there.

Witch's Advice

*(Whispering into the reader's ear in a low voice,
as though horrified.)*

Try not to laugh
first thing in the morning!

Don't listen to the trees
guarding the paths!

Don't give away your name
to the somnolent earth
till midnight has struck!

To the snow and the rain
don't offer your hand!

Only open your window
for the smaller planets
with which you are familiar!

Letting you into the secret:
a quiet word to a customer,
mistrust mistrust!
You never know what might happen.

D

A DISEMBODIED VOICE
UNE VOIX SANS PERSONNE
(1954)

Les femmes de ménage

Le ciel c'est moi Je sais que mes pauves étoiles
par le chagrin du temps longuement attendries
vieillissent par degré Ce sont elles que je vois
silencieuses anonymes les genoux pleins de poussière
tôt le matin laver l'escalier quand je viens
accrocher aux murs gris de l'éternel Bureau
mon avare sommeil mes réserves de songe
À l'arbre qui vieillit aussi dans le jardin
j'ai dit cent fois j'ai dit mille fois: je connais
j'ai dit: je sais je me souviens c'était hier
tout l'espace! Ma vie est là dans vos ramures
ma vie est là dans les dossiers ma vie est là
qui s'en va par le téléphone et qui me parle
ma vie est là dans les portes ouvertes
sur le crépitement des lampes le soir
                                        Ah oui
vieilles vieilles étoiles, blancs cheveux poussière
femmes du pauvre ménage de l'aube
puisque c'est moi qui vous le dis je vous protège
nous vieillissons ensemble J'ai compris je sais tout
d'avance car le ciel c'est moi Il faut attendre
et se taire comme tout se tait, je vous le dis.

The Charladies

I am the heavens. I know that my poor stars
long suffering under the sorrows of time
are ageing day by day. Them do I see
unspeaking unknown knees gnarled and stained with dust
scrubbing the stairs as I come at break of day
to hang on the grey eternal Office walls
my meagre sleep the remnants of my dreams
I've said a thousand times if I've said it once
to the tree in the garden also ageing: I know
I've said: I know I remember only the day before
the whole of space! My life is lost in your leaves
my life is lost in the folders my life is there
seeping out through the telephone as it speaks
my life is lost in the gaping doors which look out
on the flickering lamps of evening
                                        Ah yes

aged aged stars dust white hair
caretakers of dawn's poor household
I tell you now I shall take care of you
together we shall grow old I understand I know all
in advance for I am the heavens Just wait a while
keep silent as all is silent I tell you now.

SPACE AND THE FLUTE
L'ESPACE ET LA FLÛTE
(1958)

VARIATIONS ON TWELVE DRAWINGS BY PICASSO
VARIATIONS SUR DOUZE DESSINS DE PICASSO

«Moi je conjure moi je convoque
en moi je fais surgir qui je veux
je suis ventre creux l'espace
batteur de batteries froides
Silence autour des objets
mèche du fouet cobra joli
le tracé du ver dans le sable
toute explosion de planète
en air de flûte finit.»

– Espace qui me suscites
serpent qui me dévores
profondeur liberté
à ton signal j'accours
à ton signal je meurs
puisque tu es la Danse
je pleurerai dans ton rire
je m'éteindrai dans ta robe
ma cendre même a son dessin.

'I conjure I convoke
summon whom I will within myself
I am empty belly I am space
drummer on frigid drums
Silence surrounding objects
whip's lash cobra's beauty
worm's track traced in the sand
planets' explosions all
end in a melody played on the flute.'

– Space which calls me forth
serpent devouring me
depths my freedom
at your signal I come running
at your signal I fade away
since you are dance
I shall weep within your laughter
I shall die within your robe
my very cinders have their line.

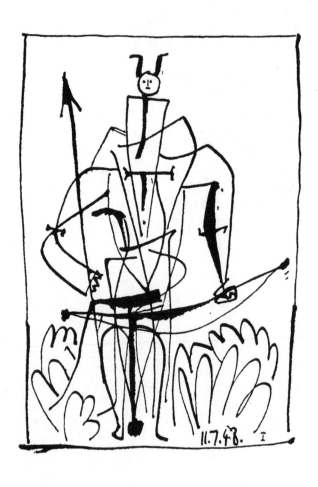

1

J'inscris dans l'homme la force et le repos
le berger les bêtes cornues
la lance l'arc et la flèche
la tâche violente et
là-haut la tête étroite et cruelle
de l'insecte guerrier. J'inscris
la danse repliée sur son espace
et dans le silence qui s'accroît
le tremblement de la Musique
J'inscris
Je signifie
Je distribue
Je donne l'ordre
mais j'obéis au cadre de la vie
à la mesure de l'œil.

*

In man I inscribe strength and repose
the shepherd the horned beasts
the spear the bow the arrow
the violent task and
at the top the tiny cruel head
of a warlike insect. I inscribe
dance doubled back upon its space
and in the gathering silence
the quavering of Music
I inscribe
I signify
I distribute
I order
but comply with life's frame
and eye's measure.

2

Le peintre enroule déroule
plie détord aplatit
casse éparpille effiloche
fronce festonne tortille
tache taraude ravaude
installe accroche répartit
étire boucle débrouille
désigne lance, – et s'en va.

Le poète déglutit
mâche goûte humecte mord
râcle rumine ronchonne
ronge siffle serine
lappe susurre murmure
savoure salive entonne
grogne grince décortique
attise souffle – et se tait.

*

The painter rolls unrolls
folds disentangles flattens
flounces scallops twists
stains screw-taps patches
installs hangs allots
stretches loops unravels
points casts – and leaves.

The poet gulps
gustates chomps licks bites
scrapes ruminates grumbles
gnaws hisses tootles
laps whispers murmurs
savours salivates strikes up
grunts grates skins
fans breath – and is silent.

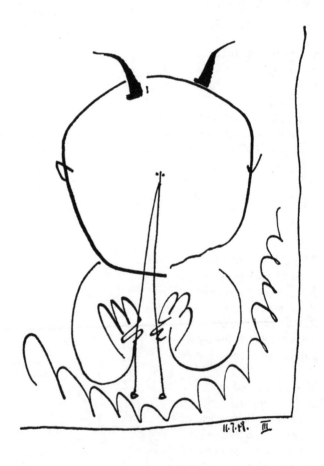

3

Voyez ma main elle a des doigts
rapide comme le paraphe
double comme ma flûte et ma corne
elle a fait reculer mes yeux
dans le volume de silence
qu'emplit la ruse de mes joues.

*

See my hand has fingers
quick as a flourish
twofold like my flute and horns
it has made my eyes recede
into the volume of silence
swelled by the guile of my cheeks.

4

En tricotant des doigts le flûtiau naïf
a fait naître un lion grand comme le soleil
C'était dans la splendeur de l'Arcadie
les troupeaux se perdaient sous les amples sourcils

Regarde cette Face où nous demeurons tous
lents comme l'horizon et dessinant les traits
d'une colère qui se prolonge.

*

With fingers' play the naive flageolet
gave birth to a lion large as the sun
This in the midst of Arcadian splendours
and flocks would be lost in the bushing of these brows

Regard that Face wherein we all reside
like the horizon lingering and drawing the lines
of a lasting anger.

5

Liseron de mon cœur
sirène de mes cornes
supplice de ma flèche
toton de mon fouet
fille de mon flûtiau
de part en part je te perce.

Vive le dessin qui m'arrache
à mes ombres par le ciel
car ce pastoral sujet
(sauf pour le plaisir d'un mot
ti-ô flûtiau ti-ô ti-ô)
ne m'est pas habituel.

*

Bindweed to my heart
siren to my horns
martyr to my arrow
top to my whip
daughter to my flageolet
through and through I pierce you.

Power to the line which snatches me
by the sky from my shadows
for (were it not the pleasure of a word
o-lay flageolet o-lay o-lay)
I find this pastoral subject
unfamiliar.

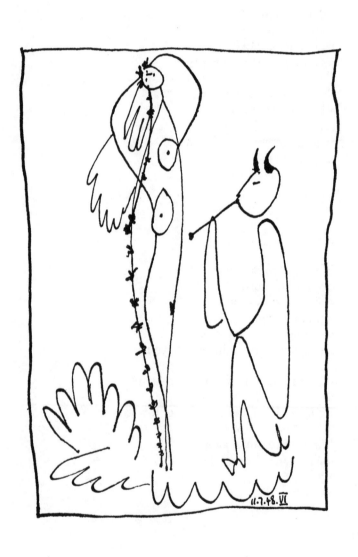

6

Les jambes? – soulignent.
La bouche? – mérite.
La danseuse? – elle est.

Le serpent? – dessine.
Le fouet? – anime.
La flûte? – fleurit.

L'espace? – dispose.
Le monde? – s'absente.
Le son? – apparaît.

*

Legs? – underline.
Mouth? – merits.
Dancer? – is.

Snake? – draws.
Whip? – quickens.
Flute? – flowers.

Space? – disposes.
World? – disappears.
Sound? – appears.

7

Sous les plumes d'autruche
des feuillages faciles
une dame d'espalier
toute de boucles cousue
comme au tuteur préparée
de seins d'enfant attifée
sur elle-même penchée
à la pointe de ma flûte
danse en l'honneur d'ume joue
que d'un seul trait le jour gonfle.

*

Under the ostrich plumes
of facile foliage
an espaliered lady
scrolled in hoops
already staked out
bedecked with childlike breasts
leans back on herself
at the tip of my flute
and dances in honour of a cheek
swollen by daylight in a single line.

8

C'était au temps heureux où je paissais
dans les prairies de l'avenir
Sur les champs dépassés
je me retournais parfois
avec tendresse et mélancolie.
Or, la menace était loin devant moi
mais c'est cela qui peu à peu
rendait ma démarche plus pesante.

*

It was in those happy days when I grazed
in the meadows of the future
With tenderness and with sadness
I sometimes turned back
on the fields left behind.
Now the threats were far before me
but little by little
this it was that turned my steps to lead.

9

Des chiffres plein les corbeilles
des fifres plein les oreilles
deux cornes dans le soleil

Des lignes pour séparer
pour décorer pour sonner
des plumes pour les bergers

Pour la distance deux touffes
pour le sol un feston
je suis angle toi boucle
tu es biche moi bouc
le paysage bouge
chalumeau tympanon.

*

Baskets laden with cyphers
ears resounding with fifers
two horns in the sun

Lines to separate
to decorate to resound
plumes for the shepherds

Two wisps for the distance
a garland for the ground
I am angle you are hoop
you are hind and I am goat
the landscape moves
reed-pipe and dulcimer.

10

À la turque le satyre
en tailleur le faune
face à face pour le jeu
Pan dans la flûte et le chalumeau!

Les serpents de vos ronds de jambe
et vos yeux aigus obliques
par la hauteur attirés
vers la pointe des sons s'élancent
images de vos cornes.

Un seul trait sans ombre
au doigt du créateur
vous tire du néant

Un jour ainsi je coulerai sur les choses
ruban par la voix proféré
un seul parfait docile interminable mot.

*

Cross-legged the satyr
saltirewise the faun
face to face in play
Pan in the flute and the reed-pipe.

The snaking curves of your obeisance
and your narrow slanting eyes
attracted by the height
leap upwards to the sounds' peak
images of your horns.

A single unshaded line
at the point of the creator's finger
draws you from the void

One day thus shall I wind around things
a ribbon proffered by the voice
a single unending perfect docile word.

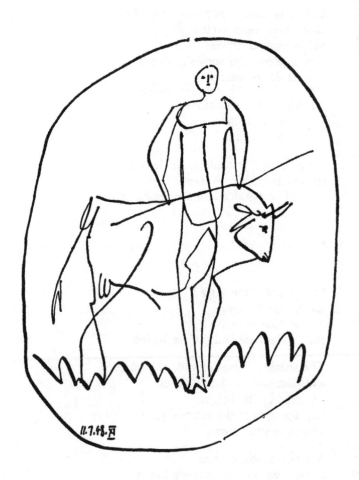

11

Comme du fond de l'eau
comme du fond des âges
sous les arches du ciel
je vois à l'horizon
grandir réconciliés
le bouvier le taureau.

C'était bien avant le supplice
O songe éveillé tu retrouves
piqués sur la prairie
la corne l'aiguillon
l'innocence oubliée
sous le sable et la cendre
les veines de l'espace
le sillage du vent.

*

As though from depths of water
As though from depths of time
beneath the arches of the sky
I see rise against the horizon
in reconciliation
the herdsman and the bull.

It was well before the torture
O waking dream you rediscover
pinned to the meadow
the horn the goad
the forgotten innocence
beneath the sand and the cinders
the veins of space
the wake of the wind.

12

Aimer d'amour ce que l'on tue
en tracer le portrait pour les siècles
ô pur profil par la mort ennobli
de la victime aux yeux de femme
animal-dieu crucifié
gravé dans la poussière
par le couteau du soleil!

Ah qui viendra nous délivrer
de la naissance et de la mort
par quoi tout crime est justifié?
Laissez-moi aimer sans détruire
le tendre museau des bêtes
Je suis dans le troupeau je regarde j'admire
la profondeur du jour.

*

To love with true love what you kill
trace its portrait for centuries to come
o pure profile ennobled by death
of the victim with woman's eyes
animal-god crucified
engraved in dust
by the knife of the sun!

Oh who will come to deliver us
from birth and from death
by which all crimes are justified?
Let me love and not destroy
the delicate muzzle of beasts
within the herd I stand I look admire
the depths of daylight.

E

ÉPILOGUE I

Après avoir effacé
tout ce que d'ombre promet
le sifflement qui me charme
après avoir en ce lieu –
Marsyas clown ou couleuvre –
rejeté toute ma vie
l'horizon clarté n'entend
volumes crevés outres vides
que le très doux glissement
d'une même ligne longue
·qui me lie à la surface

Silence ailleurs qu'en moi seul
de rien je gonfle ma joue
dans le signe que je trace
tout l'espace est donné.

ÉPILOGUE II

Mon théâtre sans ombre
cette flûte qui parle
ma vie au grand complet
pour vous pour vous connaître
il me suffit du jour
(le vent sur mes prairies
pâlit les noirs pavots
échappés de l'enfer)

Elle existe la joie
sans arme elle demeure
depuis les premiers temps
elle est là pour nous tous
elle franchit l'espace
le grand jour lui suffit
qui tourne autour des choses
comme un air de chanson.

EPILOGUE I

Having effaced
all that promise of shadow
offered by the charmer's piping
having here rejected –
Marsyas clown or grass-snake –
the whole of my life
the horizon brightness implies
exploded volumes empty winesacks
only the very gentle slide
of a single extended line
linking me to the surface

Silence elsewhere than within myself
I swell my cheek with the void
in the sign which I trace
is given the whole of space.

EPILOGUE II

My unshaded theatre
this speaking flute
my life spread out
before you to know you
for me daylight suffices
(over my meadows the wind
whitens the black poppies
escaped from Hell)

Joy exists
unarmed it has endured
from the beginning of time
it is there for us all
traversing space
for it broad daylight suffices
winding about things
like the air of a song.

TALES OF OBSCURITY
HISTOIRES OBSCURES
(1961)

Le jeune homme et la mer

La mer s'enfuyait devant lui
avec sa traîne de dentelles bruissantes
emportant ses bijoux ses voiles ses cailloux.

Il courut d'abord vivement
joyeusement, le vent du large
entrait dans ses poumons. Mais la frange d'écume
toujours courait un peu plus loin,
menu murmure d'ironie.

Comme un chasseur à la poursuite
d'une bête démesurée
il courut il courut longuement longuement
jusqu'à perdre le souffle et gagner le délire.
Le soir était tombé. Vint la nuit. Mais les vagues
avaient continué leur fuite dans le vent.
On eût dit que la mer
avait oublié sa coutume
son rythme son repos ses soupirs ses marées.
Alors il courut haletant,
le cœur sur le point de se rompre,
le front près d'éclater, les pieds en sang.
Mais toujours mais toujours l'horizon reculait
et dans les astres se plongeait.

La nuit passa puis vint la première aube
une seconde nuit un second jour
et pendant douze jours et douze nuits
pour atteindre la mer il courut vainement.

Un soir cette plage sans fin
peu à peu descendant les rampes du soleil
l'entraîna jusqu'au fond des fosses bourdonnantes
d'un grand théâtre abandonné
où des foules de gens
en habits d'apparat couverts de coquillages
chantaient sans voix, dormant debout.

The Young Man and the Sea

The sea fled before him
with its train of rustling lace
embarking its jewels its sails its stones.

At first he ran lightly
quickly, the high sea wind
filling his lungs. But the fringe of spray
ran always further
minimal ironic murmurings.

Like a hunter at the chase
in pursuit of an enormous beast
he ran he ran long and fast and hard
till he lost his breath and his head began to swim.
Dusk had fallen. Night came on. But the waves
continued to flee into the wind.
You might have thought that the sea
had forgotten its customs
its rhythm its repose its sighs its tides.
So panting on he ran,
heart at breaking point,
forehead near to bursting, feet clotted with blood.
But still the horizon continued to recede
and plunge into the stars.

Night passed then came the first dawn light
a second night and then a second dawn
and for twelve long days and twelve long nights
to reach the sea he ran in vain.

And then one evening
that measureless beach
stepping slowly down the staircase of the sun
led him to the bottom of the droning pit
of a huge abandoned theatre
where crowds of people
in shell-studded festive robes
sang voiceless songs asleep and yet erect.

Quand les premiers accords sonnèrent dans l'orchestre,
alors la mer cessa de fuir devant cet homme
et sur lui referma lentement
sa robe immense et maternelle
et l'odeur de l'amour et le bruit des cailloux.

When the first chords were struck in the orchestra
then the sea abandoned its flight
and slowly enfolded him
in its enormous maternal mantle
in the odour of love and the sound of stones.

THE SHADOW'S SHARE
LA PART DE L'OMBRE
(1972)

Grilles et balcons
(à la mémoire de mon père)

J'ai souvent contemplé avec angoisse, dans les rues anciennes de Paris, plus d'une étrange façade sans voix; mais toujours comme autant de réponses, mes yeux rencontraient, aux fenêtres, maints vieux balcons de fer forgé où résiste et résonne à mille pluies l'antique volonté de tracer des signes.

Brusquement, pour moi seul, ces trésors perdus, ces lingots noirs remontaient au jour à travers l'amoncellement glauque des années; comme eux, par notre dialogue muet, j'étais sauvé, car la peur des mélanges indistincts, des masses ensevelies m'attire vers ces écheveaux débrouillés et la peur des fluides vers ces appuis sonores.

*

Tout ce qui est *inscrit* fascine notre regard: une veine dans la pierre, le sillon laissé dans une écorce par le grignotement d'un ver, les nervures d'une feuille, le bord éclairé d'une colline.

Avec quelle avidité l'œil appréhende un signe, un simple contour ou un réseau et avec quelle gourmandise (avec une patience d'insecte), il suit chaque trait, passe d'un point au plus proche, se lève, s'abaisse, tourne à gauche, à droite, revient sur ses pas, hésite, palpe et repart en glissant! Devant tout aspect arrêté du monde, l'œil éprouve au plus haut la joie de son propre mouvement, la LECTURE!

Se débarrasser du plus lourd, se confier au plus ténu; feindre que les objets les plus grands, les plus opaques, les plus pesants soient contenus dans un filet de mailles sans épaisseur, afin de pouvoir les utiliser plus sûrement, les mesurer, les comparer, détacher d'eux cette mince pellicule de lignes que l'on peut déplier ou tordre à sa guise: tel est notre plaisir et notre ruse.

*

Ainsi, pour nous donner à lire, le forgeron rivait les barres d'un balcon et, magnanime, offrait cet appui à des bras qui, tour à tour, sont tombés en poussière. Mais lui demeure auprès et si, d'une clé, je heurte les fers qu'il frappait, j'entends encor, dans leur son resté

Grilles and Balconies
(to the memory of my father)

I have often contemplated with anxiety, in the old streets of Paris, many a strange voiceless façade; but each time, as though in response to my gaze, my eyes would meet, in front of the windows, old balconies in wrought-iron, within which the ancient will to trace signs resounds and resists through a thousand rainstorms.

Suddenly, for me alone, these lost treasures, these black ingots would struggle back upwards towards the daylight through the murky random heaps of the years. Like these treasures, I would be saved by our mute dialogue, for the fear of indistinct clutter and buried masses draws me towards these unravelled skeins, and fear of the fluid towards these sonorous supports.

*

Everything *inscribed* fascinates our gaze; the lode in a rock, the trace left in the skin of a fruit by the gnawing of a worm, the veins in a leaf, the light on the edge of a hill.

With what avidity does the eye apprehend a sign, whether it be a simple contour or a web of tracery, and with what gluttony (what insect-like patience) it follows every line, passes from one point to the next, looks up, looks down, turns to the left, to the right, comes back on its steps, hesitates, feels, and slides onwards! Before every sharply defined aspect of the world the eye experiences to the full the joy of its own movement, READING!

To free ourselves from what is most heavy, to trust to what is most tenuous, to make as though the largest, most opaque and weighty objects were contained within a network composed of links lacking in substance, to be able to use them with more certainty, to measure them, compare them, to peel off that thin film of lines which can be unfolded or twisted at will: that is our pleasure and our ruse.

*

Thus, for our reading, the blacksmith riveted the rails of a balcony and, magnanimously, offered it as a support for arms which one after the other have fallen to dust. But the blacksmith is still close by, and if I tap with a key the iron which he beat in the past, I can

141

pur, jaillir du fond des siècles criminels, le cri de son effort et de son triomphe.

Il avait appris à former toutes les figures: les *anses*, les *graines*, les *fleurons*, les *consoles*, les *enroulements*, les *rinceaux*. Rappelons à notre esprit reconnaissant ces enchanteurs du fer, qui ont façonné à la flamme un langage si parfait qu'ils n'ont pas même éprouvé la nécessité de lui imposer un «sens» particulier. Éternellement indéchiffrables, ces chiffres sont sauvés de l'erreur.

J'emporte dans ma mémoire tant de lignes persuasives. Je les pose partout autour de moi et reconnais en tremblant de joie qu'elles sont faites à l'image des contours de tout ce qui est. Par elles, je vois le monde s'éclaircir et tout me devient pénétrable.

*

J'ai besoin de savoir que tout n'est pas confondu. Je crains d'étouffer. Je redoute autant le déferlement laiteux du matin par les fenêtres que l'encombrement de la nuit. Je me répands et me divise: JE VOIS, JE TOUCHE ET ME SOUVIENS.

Si nul objet n'est préservé du danger de fondre et s'il est un feu qui vient à bout de tout, rien d'autre ne peut me rassurer que le CONTOUR, qui brise et sépare et vengera de son fouet les pires métamorphoses. Tant que je serai là pour le suivre, ce fil souple, indéfiniment capable de figures, saisira dans ses rets tout ce qui vient de naître ou de mourir: la cendre même aura son dessin.

*

Vous êtes donc encore plus forts que je ne croyais, barreaux des grilles, balcons qui me tenez. Je me penche sans crainte pour voir passer un monde de nuages. Ce fer, quand mon esprit le tire de sa source cachée, redevient incandescent et coule en rigoles de flammes, nettes et définies, sur l'air et le sol indistincts. Mais à la rencontre furieuse de cette fange et de ce sol chargés d'eau, il se fige, implacable, et se resserre sur chaque objet. C'est le moment pour nous, disciples de ses premiers maîtres, de le tordre, de le plier ou de l'écraser, de le conduire dans nos veines ou de le suivre sur les canaux qu'il creuse entre les choses, pour que tout, enfin, PRENNE FORME!

still hear in its unsullied sound, surging from the depths of centuries of crime, the cry of his effort and his triumph.

He had learned to form all the figures: the *graines* the *fleurons*, the *consoles*, the *volutes*, the *foliated scrolls*. Let us recall to our grateful minds those iron-charmers who fashioned with flame a language so perfect that they never even felt the need to impose on it a particular "sense". Eternally indecipherable, these cyphers are proof against error.

I carry away in my memory so many persuasive lines. I place them all around me, and recognise, trembling with joy, that they are made in the image of the contours of all that is. Through them, the world's darkness is lightened and all for me becomes penetrable.

*

I need to know that everything is not confused. I am afraid of stifling. I fear as much the milky unfurling of the morning in the window-panes as the congestion of the night. I spread myself and am divided: I SEE, I TOUCH, I REMEMBER.

If no object can be protected from the danger of melting, and if there is a fire which nothing can resist, then nothing can reassure me but the CONTOUR, which breaks, separates and avenges with its lash the most awful of metamorphoses. So long as I am there to follow it, that flexible thread, indefinitely capable of forming figures, will capture in its net all that has just been born or just died: ash itself will have its design.

*

Thus you are stronger than I had thought, bars and traceries, balconies which hold me. I lean over without fear to watch the passing of a world of clouds. This iron, when my mind draws it from its hidden source, becomes once more incandescent and trickles in rivulets of flame, clear and distinct, onto the indefinite air and earth. But, on its furious contact with this waterlogged mud and soil it sets implacably and takes a grip on each object. And this is the moment for us, the disciples of its original masters, to twist it, bend it, or flatten it, to conduct it into our veins or to follow it along the channels which it gouges between things, so that everything, finally, TAKES FORM!

FORMERIES
FORMERIES
(1976)

Interrogation et négation

Vous? Moi?
Non, personne
personne jamais
non vraiment personne jamais.

Comment? Ni où,
ni quoi,
ni comment?

Non vraiment personne jamais
nulle part
rien ni personne
jamais
non jamais
jamais jamais jamais
jamais
jamais
non, jamais.

Interrogative and Negative

You? Me?
No, no one
no one never
no really no one never.

What? Not nowhere
nor nothing
nor no way?

No really no one never
nowhere
nothing and no one
never
no never
never never never
never
never
no, never.

Sons en S

La Saveur
la Sévérité
le Souffle

Le Séjour
le Secret
la Suie

Je rejette le Soleil le
Supplice le Serpent le
Sarcophage Socrate Samson
Sisyphe et caetera en
tas dans un coin de
la page.

Épithètes

Une source – corrompue
Un secret – divulgué
Une absence – pesante
Une éternité – passagère
Des ténèbres – fidèles
Des tonnerres – captifs
Des flammes – immobiles
La neige – en cendre
La bouche fermée
Les dents serrées
La parole niée
muette
bourdonnante
glorieuse
engloutie.

Sounds in S

Savour
Severity
Suspiration

Sojourn
Secret
Soot

> I reject Sun
> Suffering Serpent
> Sarcophagus Socrates Samson
> Sisyphus and so on and
> leave them in a heap in a
> corner of the page

Epithets

A spring – tainted
A secret – divulged
An absence – weighty
An eternity – fleeting
Shades – faithful
Thunderbolts – captive
Flames – steadfast
Snow – in ashes
Mouth – closed
Teeth – clenched
Word – denied
mute
mumbling
swaggering
swallowed.

Verbe et Matière

J'ai je n'ai pas
J'avais eu je n'ai plus
J'aurai toujours

*Un béret Un cheval de bois Un
jeu de construction Un père
Une mère Les taches de soleil à
travers les arbres Le chant du
crapaud la nuit Les orages de
septembre.*

J'avais je n'ai plus
Je n'aurai plus jamais

*Le temps de grandir, de dési-
rer. L'eau glacée tirée du puits
Les fruits du verger Les œufs
frais dans la paille. Le grenier
La poussière Les images de
femmes dans une revue légère
Les gifles à l'heure du piano
Le sein nu de la servante.*

Si j'avais eu
J'aurais encore

*La fuite nocturne dans les astres
La bénédiction de l'espace
L'adieu du monde à travers la
clarté La fin de toute crainte de
tout espoir L'aurore démas-
quée Tous les pièges détruits
Le temps d'avant toutes choses.*

Verb and Matter

I have I have not
I had had I have no more
I shall always have

> *A beret A rocking horse A Meccano set A
> father A mother Dappled sunlight
> through the trees The night-time song of
> the toad the storms of September.*

I had I have no more
I shall never have again

> *Time to grow, to desire. Cool water drawn
> from the well Fruit from the orchard Fresh
> eggs in straw The hayloft Dust Pictures of
> girls in a dirty magazine A slap on the face
> in the piano lesson The maid's naked
> breast.*

If I had had
I would still have

> *Nocturnal flight to the stars
> The blessing of space
> Farewell to the world through light The
> end of all fear and all hope Dawn's
> unmasking The dismantling of all traps
> Time before All.*

Mortel battement

Ici commence et meurt
le peut-être encore
le très-peu le presque pas

Nulle image. Rien à voir
ni le clair ni l'obscur ni la couleur
l'ombre un instant gardée
d'un objet disparu

C'est que les signes tracés
aussitôt le feu les flambe:
il roule en deçà des sons
un grondement monotone

À travers l'énorme rien
la menace du possible
avec l'impossible
se cache pour s'accoupler

Par un bruit de paroles
je m'efforce d'imiter
ce mortel battement
qui couvre le silence.

Life and Death Beats

Here begins and here dies
that which might yet be
the minimal the hardly there

No image. Nothing to be seen
no light no shade no colour
the shadow fleetingly retained
of a vanished object

For once signs are traced
they burst at once in flames:
this side of sounds
rolls a rumbling monotony

Across the enormity of the void
the threat of the possible
sneaks off and pairs off
with what is impossible

I create a din of words
trying to imitate
those beats of life and death
which cover silence.

Un chemin

Un chemin qui est un chemin
sans être un chemin
porte ce qui passe
et aussi ce qui ne passe pas

Ce qui passe est déjà passé
au moment où je le dis
Ce qui passera
je ne l'attends plus je ne l'atteins pas

Je tremble de nommer les choses
car chacune prend vie
et meurt à l'instant même
où je l'écris.

Moi-même je m'efface
comme les choses que je dis
dans un fort tumulte
de bruits, de cris.

A Way

A way which is a way
without being a way
bears what passes
and what does not come to pass

What passes is past
even as I name it
For what will come to pass
I do not wait I cannot reach it

I fear to name things
they come to life
and die the moment
I write them down.

Myself I erase
like the things I name
in an unholy din
of sounds and screams.

Petite flamme

Petite flamme t'éteindras-tu?
– Oui s'il pleut s'il vente

Et s'il fait beau?
– Le soleil suffit, rien ne brille

Et s'il fait nuit?
– S'il fait nuit, dort tout le monde
On n'y voit goutte.

Donc à la fin, de toute manière
la petite flamme s'éteint.

Le temps l'horloge

L'autre jour j'écoutais le temps
qui passait dans l'horloge.
Chaînes, battants et rouages
il faisait plus de bruit que cent
au clocher du village
et mon âme en était contente.

J'aime mieux le temps s'il se montre
que s'il passe en nous sans bruit
comme un voleur dans la nuit.

Little Flame

Little flame will you die?
– Yes if rain falls and wind blows

And if the sun shines?
– If the sun shines no flame gleams

And if night falls?
– When night falls the whole world sleeps
There's nothing to be seen.

So after all, in all event
the little flame it dies.

Time the Clock

The other day I was listening
to time passing through the clock.
Chains clappers cogs
it made more noise
than a barrel-load of monkeys
in the village belfry
and my soul was glad

I'd rather keep a watch on time
than let it pass through us
like a thief in the night.

SO SO
COMME CECI COMME CELA
(1979)

Reflets sur le Lac de Garde

Ô lago ô lalago!
Ô Himmel!
Ô Himmemel!
Une barque imaginaire
sur une vague invisible

Neige dans l'air à peine vue
au flanc des monts
Regarder comme on rêve
ou comme on meurt ou comme on renaîtra

Dingen
im Niente corrente
flowers della mattina

Entre Sehen and oubli
Je fonds je fuis
je finis l'infini.

Sais-tu quel est ce temps qui passe?
Ce n'est qu'un oiseau son reflet.

Le présent comme souvenir
Ergo sum comme on espère.

Frisson degli giorni
im Ewigkeit
Nebbia sed sorriso
Orgasme with Ophelia
Venit nox sicut aurora.

Reflections on Lake Garda

O lago o lalago!
O Himmel;
O Himmemel!
An imaginary barque
on an invisible wave

Snow half glimpsed in the air
on the mountainside
See how we dream
or how we die or are reborn

Dingen
im Niente corrente
Fleurs della mattina

Between Sehen et oblivion
fluid I flee
finite make the infinite.

Do you know what time it is that passes?
It is but a bird its reflection.

The present as memory
Ergo sum as one hopes.

Frisson degli giorni
im Ewigkeit
Nebbia sed sorriso
Orgasm avec Ophélie
Venit nox sicut aurora.

F

Nouvelle énigme pour Œdipe
(Monologue à deux voix)

Est-ce que c'est une chose? – Non.
Est-ce que c'est un être vivant? – Oui.
Est-ce que c'est un végétal? – Non.
Est-ce que c'est un animal? – Oui.
Est-ce que c'est un animal rampant? – Quelquefois, pas toujours.
Comment se tient-il? – Debout.
Est-ce qu'il vole? – De plus en plus.
Est-ce que c'est un animal qui siffle? – Quelquefois.
Qui rugit qui meugle, hennit, miaule, aboie, jappe, jacasse? – Oui,
    s'il le veut, par imitation.
Est-ce qu'il sait fabriquer des nids pour ses enfants? – Il construit
    toutes sortes d'alvéoles tremblants.
Est-ce qu'il creuse des galeries souterraines? – De plus en plus parce
    qu'il vole et qu'il a peur.
Est-ce qu'il se nourrit de fruits, de plantes? – Oui parce qu'il est
    délicat.
Et de viandes? – Énormément parce qu'il est cruel.
Est-ce qu'il parle? – Beaucoup: ses paroles font un bruit infernal tout
    autour de la terre.
C'est donc le lion le tigre et en même temps le bétail et en même
    temps le perroquet le chat le chien le singe le castor et la
    taupe? – Oui oui oui oui à la fois tout cela, à la fois lui-même
    et tous les autres.
Est-ce qu'il vit la nuit ou le jour? – Il vit la nuit et le jour. Parfois il
    dort le jour et travaille la nuit parce qu'il a peur de ses rêves.
Est-ce qu'il voit, est-ce qu'il entend? – Il voit tout il entend tout, mais
    il se bouche les oreilles.
Qu'est-ce qu'il fait quand il travaille? – Il édifie de hautes murailles
    pour cacher le soleil. Il parle, il chante, il bourdonne pour
    couvrir le bruit du tonnerre.
Et quand il ne fait rien? – Il se cache. Il tremble de tous ses membres,
    il ne sait pas pourquoi.
Est-ce qu'il va vers quelque chose, vers quelqu'un? – Il le croit, il
    feint d'être appelé, désigné, couronné.
Est-il mortel? – Il pense être immortel mais il meurt.
Est-ce qu'il aime sa mort? – Il la déteste il ne la comprend pas.

New Quiz Game for Oedipus

(Monologue for two voices)

Is it a thing? – No.

Is it alive? – Yes.

Is it vegetable? – No.

Is it animal? – Yes.

Does it creep and crawl? – Sometimes, not always.

How does it stand? – Erect.

Does if fly? – More and more.

Does it whistle? – Sometimes.

Does it roar does it moo, miaow, bark, bay, whinny, chatter? – Yes,
    when it feels like it, for the sake of mimicry.

Does it know how to make nests for its children? – It builds all kinds
    of heaving hives.

Does it dig underground passages? – More and more because it flies
    and is frightened.

Does it feed on fruit and plants? – Yes because it is discerning and
    sensitive.

And on meat? – A great deal, because it is cruel and insensitive.

Does it speak? – Incessantly: its words make a hellish din all around
    the earth.

So it's the lion the tiger the cows and the bulls and also the parrot the
    cat the dog the monkey the beaver and the mole? – Yes yes
    yes yes all that at the same time itself and everything else.

Does it live by night or by day? – It lives both by night and by day.
    Sometimes it sleeps by day and works by night because it
    fears its dreams.

Can it see, can it hear? – It can see and hear everything, but it blocks
    its ears.

What does it do when it works? – It builds high walls to hide the sun.
    It talks, it sings, it murmurs and drones to cover the noise of
    thunder.

And when it's doing nothing? It hides. It shakes in all its limbs, it
    knows not why.

Is it moving towards something, towards someone? – It thinks so, it
    pretends to have been called, chosen, made lord of all it
    surveys.

Is it mortal? – It thinks it is immortal, but it dies.

Does it love death? – It abhors it and fails to comprehend it.

Que fait-il contre sa mort puisqu'il ne l'aime pas? – Il la multiplie en lui et hors de lui partout sur la terre la mer et dans les airs, il la répand à profusion il se nourrit de vie, c'est-à-dire de mort.

Et avec tout ce massacre, qu'est-ce qu'il espère gagner? – Il croit perdre de vue le terme, il brouille l'horizon.

Qu'attend-il à la fin? – Sa mort, sa propre mort.

Et lorsque vient sa propre mort? – Il ne la reconnaît pas: il croit que c'est la vie et il se prosterne en pleurant.

Since it does not love death, what does it do to combat it? – It does all it can to increase its sway, within itself and beyond itself, through land, sea and air, it spreads it lavishes it, feeds on life, that is, on death.

And what does it hope to gain by all this slaughter? – It hopes to lose sight of the end, it seeks to blur the horizon.

So finally what does it hope for? – Death, its own death.

And when that death finally comes? – It fails to recognise it: it takes it for life, goes down on bended knees and weeps.

THE TOWERS OF TREBIZOND
LES TOURS DE TRÉBIZONDE
(1983)

Les tours de Trébizonde
(à Marie-Laure)

De cet aquarium juché au cinquième étage de l'immeuble où évolue ma lenteur pensive et douloureuse de poisson pris à la nasse, de l'unique vitrage qui me sépare du boulevard, au-dessus du roulement continu des voitures, de cette paroi de verre qui miroite comme la surface gelée d'un lac de montagne, je vois au loin, vers le sud de Paris, s'allumer le soir, s'éteindre peu à peu la nuit, puis se déployer et prendre racine dans l'aurore, les hautes tours du «Quartier Italie».

Ces formes redoutables de notre destin sont autant de pontons construits tout exprès pour dévorer des milliers et des milliers de captifs innocents, mais elles ressemblent aussi à des banquises secrètement travaillées par les soubresauts imperceptibles d'un départ toujours différé.

Voyez! Avec l'agitation et les bruits qui augmentent, s'approche une fin de journée. Souvent sur le fond d'un ciel vert sombre, de ce ciel courroucé ou bienveillant, balafré de pâles plages de nuées, les tours les plus élevées (au nombre de quatre) commencent à jouer les phares portuaires dans l'immobile tempête urbaine.

Bien qu'elles soient presque imaginaires à force d'être anonymes et qu'elles semblent, par l'effet d'un inquiétant paradoxe dû à la distance, totalement inhabitées, elles ne cessent d'imposer leur présence, plus obsédante, plus menaçante que les pas d'un géant vorace et muet.

Tour à tour (c'est vraiment le mot!), dans la marée montante de l'obscurité, les minuscules et innombrables lanternes des fenêtres s'ouvrent, se ferment, s'ouvrent, se ferment, selon les mouvements inégaux d'une signalisation incompréhensible, de quelque énigmatique «alphabet Morse», puis, après avoir ainsi clignoté, elles s'illuminent toutes ensemble, comme si la raison de cet embrasement final n'était pas la communion obligatoire des reclus invisibles autour du repas du soir (servi à la même heure dans la cuisine des vrais pauvres et dans la salle à manger des faux riches), mais comme si ces nefs colossales, prenant conscience d'elles-mêmes, ne cherchaient qu'à éclairer les passes dangereuses de leur immobile navigation.

Pendant des années et des années, se sont nourries de ce spectacle, qui me fait peur et en même temps m'intrigue comme un problème insoluble, mes nuits de mauvais sommeil, mais aussi,

The Towers of Trebizond
(for Marie-Laure)

From this aquarium perched on the fifth floor of the building in which, like a fish caught in a lobster pot, my pensive and painful slowness turns this way and that, through the single pane which separates me from the boulevard, high above the incessant rumbling of the traffic, through the glass partition which gleams like the frozen surface of a mountain lake, I can see in the distance, towards the South of Paris, the tall tower blocks of the Place d'Italie. They light up in the evening, go out one by one at night, open up and take root in the dawn.

These fearsome forms of our destiny are prison-hulks deliberately constructed to devour thousands and thousands of innocent captives, but they are also like ice-floes insidiously eroded by the imperceptible tremors of a constantly deferred departure.

Look. With the rising bustle and noise, a day's end approaches. Often, against a background of dark green sky, that turbulent or benevolent sky, slashed with pale strands of cloud, the highest towers (four in number) start to play the role of harbour lights in the immobile urban storm.

Although their anonymity lends them an almost imaginary quality, and although they seem, by some paradoxical and disturbing effect of distance, to be completely uninhabited, they ceaselessly impose their presence, more obssessive and threatening than the steps of a mute voracious giant.

Towering in turn, in the rising tide of darkness, the myriad tiny lantern-lights of the windows light up, switch off, light up, switch off, according to the irregular rhythm of some incomprehensible system of signalling, some cryptic Morse code, then, after flickering in this way, they all light up together, as though the reason for this ultimate flamboyance were not the obligatory communion of invisible prisoners round the evening meal (served at the same time in the kitchens of the true poor and in the dining-rooms of the phony rich), but as though these colossal vessels were taking cognisance of themselves, and simply seeking to illuminate the dangerous straits of their static shipping routes.

For years and years, this spectacle, frightening and intriguing as an insoluble problem, has nourished my sleepless nights, as well as my nights of enchanted and fascinated insomnia, for (especially in summer) these vertiginous structures, which seem to consume life

bien souvent, mes veilles fascinées et ravies, car (en été surtout) ces édifices vertigineux, qui semblent consumer la vie au lieu de la protéger, se changent en girandoles de fête, en châteaux du délire, sans autre réalité apparente que les points d'or qui les arrachent à la nuit. On dirait que leur pavoisement désordonné efface, ou rend soudain le support monumental de leur structure plus mince, plus fragile et plus flottant qu'une nappe secouée.

Demain, selon la coutume délicate du ciel parisien, je verrai les teintes successives du matin se fondre l'une dans l'autre, passer du rose tendre au gris bleuté, rivalisant, sur les bords de cette périphérie sans espoir, avec le rêve coloré des peintres les plus gourmands de saveurs et de nuances; dès l'aube, ces vaisseaux, pris dans les vagues mortes du macadam, s'efforceront d'oublier leur sort et de sourire, lorsque leur face encore plongée dans l'ombre coupe, le long d'une arête verticale pareille à une falaise, la face offerte à la douceur du levant. Plus tard, s'étant fondues, vaporisées dans l'irradiation de la clarté solaire, puis, quelques heures après, s'étant, comme j'ai dit, effacées dans leur propre illumination électrique, les tours disparaissent enfin, absorbées par le silence de l'éloignement. Seule, alors, en pleine nuit, une vigie, pas plus grosse qu'un timbre collé en haut d'une enveloppe, quelque part sur l'abrupte paroi, révèle encore leur pesante masse endormie.

Au cours de mes dix ou douze années de veille, je me refuse à évaluer le nombre accru des morts qui se sont succédés, dans cet ensemble implacable du haut en bas de chaque immense columbarium – disparitions discrètes, manifestées seulement par la fermeture provisoire de l'une ou l'autre des fenêtres, petits hublots de l'asphyxie collective, étincelles furtives aussitôt suivies de leur cendre et j'ai enfin compris quel lien secret, dans le demi-sommeil de ma contemplation, ce paysage (occidental et terrestre par sa permanence aveugle, oriental et maritime par sa fantasmagorie nocturne) entretenait, au-delà des continents et des siècles, avec l'imagerie ensorcelée, évoquant la légende de saint Georges et de la princesse de Trébizonde, telle que l'a conçue Pisanello, à Vérone, pour l'église Sant'Anastasia.

Cette fresque, en partie abîmée, que l'on a, par précaution, détachée du haut mur primitif et transportée dans une chapelle voisine, mais qui a conservé l'essentiel de son pouvoir d'incantation, ce chef-d'œuvre naïf et savant, inspiré et tranquille, est de nature a provoquer, chez le spectateur émerveillé que je suis, une rêverie multiple et sans fin.

Je remarque d'abord que le tableau lui-même tient dans une

rather than protect it, become festive chandeliers, mad dream-like castles, with no other apparent reality than the specks of gold which snatch them from the night. It is as though their ragged bunting effaced the monumental pedestal of their structure, or suddenly rendered it more diaphanous and more insubstantial than a tablecloth shaken in the wind.

Tomorrow, following the refined customs of the Parisian sky, I shall watch the successive morning tints blend with each other, passing from a soft pink to a greyish blue, rivalling, on the fringes of these outskirts beyond hope, the coloured dreams of those painters who most relish savours and nuances; at break of day these vessels, caught in the lifeless waves of the tarmac, will try to forget their fate and smile, when the surface still bathed in shadow, cuts along a cliff-like vertical axis the surface offered to the gentle rising sun. Later, melted and evaporated into the torrents of sunlight, having been, as I said before, wiped out by their own electric illumination, the towers finally disappear, absorbed into the silence created by distance. Then, solitary in the midst of the darkness, a warning light, no larger, on the sheer concrete face, than a postage stamp stuck onto an envelope, continues to reveal their sleeping weighty mass.

In the course of my ten or twelve years of watchfulness I refuse to count the gathering number of successive deaths in the implacable blank block of each columbarium – discreet disappearances marked only by the temporary closing of one of the windows, tiny portholes in the collective asphyxia, furtive sparks immediately followed by their own ashes – and I have finally come to understand the secret links maintained in my state of semi-slumber across continents and centuries between this landscape (Western and earthbound in its blind permanence, Eastern and seaborne in its nocturnal phantasmagoria) and the enchanted imagery which depicts the legend of St George and the Princess of Trebizond, as rendered by Pisanello, in Verona, for the Church of St Anastasia.

This fresco, damaged in places, removed for protection from its original high wall, and displayed in a nearby chapel, but still retaining its essential incantatory power, this primitive and sophisticated masterpiece, tranquil in its passionate inspiration, is of a kind to trigger off in a marvelling spectator such as myself unending and multiform reveries.

First of all I notice that the picture itself is contained within a measurable space, of moderate size, whereas, by the wealth and multiplicity of its evocative suggestion, the event which it represents

surface mesurable, de moyenne grandeur, alors que, par la plénitude et la richesse des suggestions qu'il éveille, l'événement représenté semble s'étendre aux confins du monde.

Mais ce contraste entre l'espace matériel et l'espace mental ne s'arrête pas là. Dominées par un ensemble de tours fabuleuses, elles aussi étrangement désertes, toutes les figures peintes plongent dans un élément hors du temps, dans un bain de stupeur comparable à cette impression d'attente angoissée que nous éprouvons à l'approche d'un orage.

C'est sans doute la volonté, consciente et singulièrement subtile, de provoquer en nous un tel sentiment (on le retrouve dans d'autres œuvres du même artiste) qui a conduit Pisanello à maintenir ses couleurs dans une sorte de sourdine somptueuse, dans une gamme de modulations voilées, entre l'argent terni et les chamarrures noir et or, où affleurent çà et là les rondeurs luisantes de l'ivoire. (Si, comme il est vraisemblable, cette atténuation est due en partie aux intempéries et aux moisissures, on peut aussi supposer que l'harmonie générale de la fresque, telle qu'elle était perçue à l'origine, était analogue à celle d'aujourd'hui, mais dans une tonalité plus sonore, avec des détails aux couleurs plus vives et plus aiguës.)

Quant aux attitudes des personnages de drame (décor et animaux compris), ce ne sont partout que départs retardés, gestes en arrêt, mouvements amorcés et tout à coup bloqués, suspendus entre la menace d'un cataclysme imminent et la mémoire d'un temps mythique. On pourrait supposer que le peintre, en équilibre entre ses deux sollicitations majeures, entre la précision de la vérité naturaliste qui ouvre la Renaissance et la nostalgie, déjà surannée, de la fable médiévale, a voulu nous glisser dans la main la clé perdue des symboles, dont le secret est peut-être de nous faire revivre «à la demande» les phases toujours les mêmes et cependant toujours rajeunies d'un rituel à la fois magique et sacré.

*

Là, debout, face à nous, il vient d'arriver, ce jeune homme songeur qui est un saint, mais aussi un guerrier. Sa forte jambe droite, gainée d'une cotte de mailles, fait un pas décidé vers son coursier – et déjà son bras gauche pose la selle sur le dos du cheval blanc, dont nous ne voyons que la croupe énorme, sanglée dans un harnachement de cuir doré.

Il est accouru, le front ceint d'une couronne de boucles blondes,

seems to stretch to the limits of the earth.

But this contrast between material space and mental space does not stop there. Dominated by a collection of fabulous towers, which are also strangely deserted, all the painted figures are plunged into a timeless element, bathed in a stupor comparable to that feeling of anguished anticipation that we sense in face of an approaching storm.

It is doubtless the conscious and extraordinarily subtle will to create in us this kind of sensation (a similar phenomenon is to be found in other works by the same artist), that led Pisanello to work in sumptuously muted tones, to restrict himself to a scale of veiled modulations, somewhere between tarnished silver and gaudy blacks and golds, with hints, here and there of the lustrous plenitude of ivory. (If, as it seems probable, this attenuation of colour is partly due to the effects of time and damp, it is also possible to imagine that the overall harmony of the fresco, as it was originally perceived, was similar to that of today, but in a more sonorous key and with details in livelier and sharper colours.)

The postures of the actors in the drama (background and animals included), all consist but of arrested departures, frozen gestures, movements inaugurated and then suddenly blocked, suspended between the threat of an imminent cataclysm and the memory of a mythical epoch. You might imagine that the painter, caught between his two major forces of attraction, between the concern for precise naturalistic truth which characterises the beginning of the Renaissance and an already outdated nostalgia for medieval fable, wanted to slip into our hand the lost key to those symbols whose secret is perhaps their capacity to make us relive "on demand" the unchanging yet constantly renewed phases of a magic and sacred ritual.

*

There, just arrived, upright, facing us, the pensive young man who is a saint but also a warrior. His strong right leg, encased in chain-mail, steps forcefully towards his steed – and his left arm is already placing the saddle on the white horse's back, of which we can see only the enormous croup, girded with gilded leather harness.

He has come running, forehead wreathed with a crown of blond curls, his large feminine eyes turned in the direction of the dragon (but not yet looking at it for fear of being enfeebled by dread). His pug-nosed reflective face expresses determination, acceptance of

ses grands yeux de femme tournés du côté du Dragon (mais sans le regarder encore, de peur d'être affaibli par l'horreur). Sa face camuse et réfléchie exprime la détermination, la fatalité acceptée, la certitude invincible, mais elle est aussi le visage même de la tristesse, car il est triste de tuer, même un monstre, même un dragon de sang et de feu et de répondre au défi des puissances maléfiques pour confirmer, selon les mystères d'une contradiction sans remède, la suprématie de la Foi.

Bien qu'il se soit mis en route pour cette périlleuse et longue randonnée jusqu'aux rives de la mer Noire (au-delà de l'eau glauque et du ciel bleu pâle, il semble que l'on aperçoive une sombre montagne) et bien qu'il connaisse les charges de sa mission surhumaine – la délivrance d'une jeune princesse offerte en sacrifice à la mort la plus affreuse – il ne daigne même pas tourner les yeux vers la tendre victime promise. C'est comme si le drame ne concernait que nous seuls, nous qui sommes perdus dans le futur, spectateurs frissonnants rassemblés devant la scène de ce monde.

La Princesse, de son côté, par l'élégance insouciante de son maintien, paraît absente de la tragédie qui la menace directement. La venue de son défenseur a-t-elle, en un instant, effacé toute crainte sur son visage lisse et enfantin? Ou bien, non prévenue de ce qui l'attend, s'est-elle crue invitée, ce jour-là comme un autre, au grand tumulte féodal des matins de chasse? Ou bien encore est-elle déjà morte et, aussitôt ressuscitée, a-t-elle pris pour toujours le masque léger de l'innocence et de l'oubli?

On la voit de profil, elle n'est séparée de Lui que par la largeur d'un cheval. Son front, sommé d'une masse de cheveux rejetés en arrière, serrés dans les entrelacs d'épaisses cordelettes brunes, est éclairé par le globe de l'œil: un mince éclat de porcelaine blanche qui attire notre regard sur le sien et le sien sur saint Georges. Son manteau de teinte foncée, rehaussé d'hermine, étend sur le sol sa traîne aux nombreux replis, tout près d'un cavalier casqué au visage enfoui dans l'ombre du heaume, une énorme lance à son poing: il dirige vers nous la tête, fine comme un violon, de son cheval mauve et gris dont le profond regard, noir de toute la noirceur du pressentiment, *est analogue, par l'intensité de sa douleur et de sa mélancolie*, aux grands yeux tristes du Héros.

Elle est descendue, la jeune fille, du haut de la cité fantastique (pourtant déserte à cette heure fatale) dont on ne voit, au sommet d'une colline abrupte, derrière un repli de terrain, que les tours à l'architecture compliquée, ces tours fameuses, échappées d'un Moyen Âge irréel, ces tours dévoratrices et muettes, parentes de

fatality, invincible certitude, but it is also the visage of sadness, for it is a sad thing to kill, even a monster, even a dragon breathing fire and blood, and to take up the challenge of the powers of evil, to confirm, according to the mysteries of an irremediable contradiction, the supremacy of the Faith.

Although he has set out on this long and arduous expedition to the shores of the Black Sea (beyond the murky sea and the pale blue sky you can half glimpse the sombre form of a mountain), although he is aware of the weight of his superhuman mission – the deliverance of a young Princess offered in sacrifice to the most hideous of deaths – he does not even deign to turn his eyes towards the tender promised victim. It is as though we alone were implicated in this drama, we, lost in the future, we, trembling spectators assembled before the stage of this world.

As for the Princess, she seems, by the careless elegance of her demeanour, to be absent from the tragedy which directly threatens her. Has the arrival of her defender wiped in a second all fear from her smooth and childlike face? Or has she, uninformed of the fate which awaits her, simply thought that today, as on any other day, she was invited to the bawdy feudal hubbub of the hunt? Or rather, is she already dead, and, instantaneously resuscitated, has she assumed for ever the light mask of innocence and forgetfulness?

She is seen in profile, separated from him only by a horse's girth. Her forehead, crowned with a mass of pulled back hair tied up in a tracery of thick brown braids, is illuminated by the orb of her eye. A fragile gleam of white porcelain which attracts our gaze to hers and hers to St George. Her dark mantle, trimmed with ermine spreads the luxurious folds of its train on the ground, next to a casqued knight, whose face is hidden in the shadow of his helm, holding in his hand an enormous lance: he is directing towards us the delicate, violin-shaped head of his mauvish grey steed, whose profound gaze, dark with the blackness of foreboding, *is, by the intensity of its pain and melancholy, like* the huge sad eyes of the hero.

Down has come the maiden from the heights of the fantastic city (yet deserted at this fatal hour), of which you can see, at the top of a steep hill, behind a fold in the land, only the complicated architecture of the towers, those towers, fugitives from some unreal medieval epoch, those mute devouring towers, akin to the ones I peer out at anxiously on the fringes of a modern capital!

Time is suddenly contracted, images superimposed. Feudal monuments or council flats, religious or profane, Gothic or post-Cubist, these overbearing upsurges of stone or concrete, over-

celles qu'aujourd'hui je scrute avec angoisse à la périphérie d'une capitale moderne!

Le temps, subitement, se contracte, les images se superposent. Seigneuriales ou populaires, religieuses ou profanes, de style gothique ou d'inspiration cubiste, ces insolentes levées de pierre ou de ciment, qu'elles soient surchargées d'ornements sculptés ou ajourées de fenêtres toutes identiques, n'ayant, les uns et les autres, que la couleur du vent qui tourne autour d'elles, de la lumière qui les anime et du grand fleuve temporel qui les emporte on ne sait où, elles figurent, pour mon esprit effrayé, la même tentation, transmise de siècle en siècle, de revêtir d'une cuirasse (qui est, à vrai dire, un tombeau) la vulnérable et pullulante espèce des hommes, bonne pour être cueillie par les ogres insatiables dans les alvéoles des ruches citadines, comme autant de minuscules crustacés.

Justement là, à la gauche de la fresque, relégué dans le coin des rebuts et des déchets, voici le monstre affamé, sous la forme d'un énorme lézard, brun sale et pustuleux, replié sur le tas de ses proies récemment terrassées, où des biches encore vivantes, bétail mis en réserve de nourriture, côtoient les crânes humains en train de se confondre avec le sable et le roc. Il tend son abominable museau, deviné plutôt que distinct, qui, sans doute, finit de déguster la vie agonisante. Jamais n'a été formulé à ce point le contraste entre l'horreur dévastatrice qui est la loi du monde vivant et la beauté des victimes désignées, cette beauté incorruptible et hors d'atteinte qui n'est que le reflet de nos désirs exténués et le dernier recours de notre désespoir et qui pourtant se hausse au niveau souverain d'un triomphe sans récompense.

Très loin, là-bas, on aperçoit la mer, où un navire aux flancs bordés par l'écume de son sillage, à la voile arrondie par le vent, vogue de toute sa vitesse de notre côté, c'est-à-dire vers l'écueil, vers le crime et vers le naufrage. Tout auprès sont alignées, sous les portes de la ville, les faces cruelles et larges, aux regards fixes (on dit qu'ils ne sont pas de la main du maître, c'est donc qu'ils n'étaient pas dignes de lui!) de l'Empereur et de sa cour, capitaines et forbans, accompagnateurs et voyeurs fascinés qui espèrent le pire. Plus haut encore se dresse un échafaud où tournent deux pendus, déculottés selon l'usage du bourreau.

Et puis, et puis notre regard se heurte aux tours de cette cité imaginaire, fondée quand la Légende rejoignait l'Histoire, érigeant maints édifices d'un marbre ouvragé, pareils, eux aussi, à des ossements, tours de défense et de guet pour des soldats absents (ou

charged with carvings or fretted with identical windows, each reflecting only the colour of the wind winding round it, the light quickening it, and the swollen river of time which carries it to an unknown destination, are images in my unquiet mind of the same temptation, transmitted through the centuries, that of clothing with body armour (which is, if truth be told, the tomb) the swarming vulnerable human species, good for being culled by insatiable ogres in the cells of urban hives, like so many tiny crustaceous animals.

There, just there, on the left of the fresco, relegated to the corner of discarded detritus, is the affamished monster, in the shape of an enormous, pustulous, dirty-brown lizard, coiled up on the heap of its newly savaged prey, where living hinds, paddocked for future nourishment, lie side by side with human skulls almost indistinguishable from sand and rock. It proffers its fearsome muzzle, suggested rather than defined, doubtless still relishing the taste of life at the point of death. Never before has there been such an extreme expression of the contrast between the devastating horror which is the law of the living world and the beauty of the designated victims, that incorruptible and unattainable beauty which is but the reflection of our wearied desires, the supreme court of our despair, and which yet manages to raise itself to the level of a victorious final judgement with no compensation for loss.

Far away, on the other side, you can see the sea, and a boat, its flanks edged with the foam of its wake, its sails billowing in the wind, forging ahead towards our side, that is, towards reefs, crime, and shipwreck. Next to the boat, beneath the city gates, are lined up the broad cruel faces (it is claimed that they are not of the master's hand, which means they were not thought worthy of him) of the Emperor and his court, captains and corsairs, attendants and fascinated voyeurs hoping for the worst. Above them is a scaffold from which dangle two hanged men, their breeches ripped down according to the hangman's custom.

And then, then our gaze encounters the towers of this imaginary city, founded at the meeting point of Legend and History, erecting multiple edifices in highly-worked marble, also resembling whitened bones, keeps and watch-towers for absent (or perhaps hidden) soldiers, towers for the tocsin and for prayer, silent (or perhaps awaiting the moment to ring out), splendidly substituting, thanks to the enchantments of Quattrocento vision, the crenellated walls and Gothic arches brought by the Western knights for the cupolas and domes that you might expect to find in this great port on the Euxine, emancipated scion of Imperial Byzantium.

177

G

peut-être cachés), tours de tocsin et de prière qui se taisent (ou qui peut-être attendent l'heure de sonner) substituant avec splendeur, grâce aux sortilèges d'une vision du Quattrocento, les fortifications crénelées et les ogives, apportées par les chevaliers d'Occident, aux coupoles et aux dômes que l'on s'attendrait à trouver dans ce grand port du Pont-Euxin, rejeton émancipé de l'impériale Byzance.

C'est là, dans ce lieu des métamorphoses, entre hier, aujourd'hui et toujours, c'est là que, pour le bénéfice tantôt extasié, tantôt horrifié, de ce somnambulisme qui me sauve et de ces apparitions inexplicables qui m'enchantent, se sont rencontrés les tours de Trébizonde et celles (si bien nommées) de la place d'Italie, les figures rêvées et décrites par un peintre de génie avec le même soin et la même précision qu'un lévrier de meute ou un cerf debout dans la forêt, le Dragon dont la queue fait les mêmes replis que la traîne de la Princesse, les pendus et la voile du navire poussés par le même ouragan, un héros triste à mourir, la mélancolie fraternelle du cheval, la feinte indifférence de la victime et enfin, et enfin, notre sort à nous tous, passagers d'une flotte immobile, condamnée à rester, jusqu'au prochain désastre, à l'ancre dans le port, près du charnier que le monstre inassouvi, malgré la lance de saint Georges, pourvoit et accroît chaque jour.

[Paris, 1-3 février,
San Felice del Benaco, 7-20 août,
Gerberoy, 25-30 août 1983]

178

Here it is, in this place of metamorphoses, between yesterday, today and forever, here it is that for the benefit of that somnambulism, sometimes ecstatic, sometimes horrified, which saves me, and of those inexplicable apparitions which enchant me, that the towers of Trebizond and those, so aptly named, of the Place d'Italie came to meet. The figures dreamed of and depicted by a painter of genius with the same precision he would have used for a greyhound or a stag erect in the forest, the Dragon, whose tail falls in folds precisely similar to those of the Princess, the hanged men and the ship's sail moved by the same hurricane, a hero sad until death, the fraternal melancholy of the horse, the assumed indifference of the victim, and finally, finally, our common fate, passengers on an immobile fleet, condemned to remain, until the next disaster, at anchor in port, beside the charnel-house which the unassuaged monster, in spite of St George's lance, maintains and augments each day.

[Paris, 1-3 February,
San Felice del Benaco, 7-20 August,
Gerberoy, 25-30 August 1983]

Mon théâtre secret
(à Gérard Macé)

Le lieu où je me retire à part moi (quand je m'absente en société et qu'on me cherche, je suis là) est un théâtre en plein vent peuplé d'une multitude, d'où sortent, comme l'écume au bout des vagues, le murmure entrecoupé de la parole, les cris, les rires, les remous, les tempêtes, le contrecoup des secousses planétaires et les splendeurs irritées de la musique.

Ce théâtre, que je parcours secrètement depuis mes plus jeunes années sans en atteindre les frontières, a deux faces inséparables mais opposées, bref un «endroit» et un «envers», pareils à ceux d'une médaille ou d'un miroir.

De ce côté-ci, voyez comme il imite, à la perfection, l'inébranlable majesté des monuments: il semble que je puisse compter toutes les pierres, caresser de mes mains le glacis du marbre, les fractures des colonnes, la porosité du travertin...

Mais, attendez: si je fais le tour du décor (quelques pas me suffisent), alors, de l'autre côté de ces apparences pesantes, de ces voûtes et de ces murailles, mon regard tout à coup n'aperçoit plus que des structures fragiles, des bâtis provisoires et partout, dans les courants d'air et la pénombre poussiéreuse, auprès des câbles électriques entrelacés et des planches mal jointes, la toile rude et pauvre, clouée sur des châssis légers.

Telle est la loi de mon théâtre; à l'endroit, les villes et les paysages, la terre et le ciel, tout est peint, simulé à merveille. À l'envers, l'artisan de ce monde illusoire est soudain démasqué, car son œuvre, si ingénieuse soit-elle, révèle, par transparence, la misère des matériaux qui lui ont servi à édifier ses innombrables «trompe-l'œil». (Souvent je l'ai vu qui gémissait, le pinceau à la main, mêlant ses larmes à des couleurs joyeuses.) Pourtant, bien que je sois dans la confidence, je ne saurais dire où est le Vrai, car l'envers et l'endroit sont tous deux les enfants du réel, énigme qui me cerne de toutes parts pour m'enchanter et pour me perdre.

C'est sur ces échafaudages, tremblants et vides, mais très hauts, comme la voilure des trois-mâts, c'est là que se déroule, nuit et jour, l'inépuisable spectacle, sous les rafales tournantes des phares dont la source inconnue met au monde les fables qui, depuis l'enfance, m'ont nourri sans me consoler.

Ici, rien ne s'accroît ni ne diminue. L'horloge du beffroi reste au point mort, midi ou minuit, je ne sais. Les arbres ont adopté,

My Secret Theatre
(for Gérard Macé)

The place I retire to within myself (when I disappear from a social gathering, and people are looking for me, that is where I am to be found) is a windswept theatre inhabited by a multitude, from which emanate, like foam on the tips of waves, murmurings broken by words, cries, laughter, eddyings, storms, the aftermath of planetary collisions, and the nerve-wracked splendours of music.

This theatre, to which I have been slinking off in secret since my childhood without ever reaching its frontiers, has two inseparable but opposite sides, in short, an "obverse" and a "reverse", as in a medallion or a mirror.

On this side, see how it imitates to perfection the unflinching majesty of monuments: I feel I could count each stone, lovingly pass my hands over the delicate surface of the marble, the cracks in the pillars, the porous texture of the travertine.

But wait: if I walk round the set (a few steps suffice), on the other side of these weighty appearances, these vaults and walls of stone, suddenly my gaze encounters only flimsy structures, temporarily tacked together, and everywhere, in the gusts of air and the dusty twilight, amidst tangled electric cables and badly fitting boards the crude and trivial backcloth, pinned to lightweight stretchers.

This is the underlying law of my theatre: on the obverse, cities and landscapes, earth and sky, all perfectly rendered, a marvellous simulacrum. On the reverse, the artisan responsible for this world of illusion is abruptly unmasked, for his work, however ingenious, reveals through its transparency, the poverty of the means which have allowed him to erect his innumerable *trompe-l'oeil*. (Often I've seen him, sighing, brush in hand, mix his tears with bright gay colours.) And yet, although I am in on the secret, I would not know where the Truth lies, for obverse and reverse are both born of the real, and this is an enigma which encompasses me on all sides, to my delight and my confusion.

Here upon this scaffolding, hollow and rickety but very high, like the rigging of a three-master, unfolds, night and day, the endless spectacle, beneath the rotating squalls of the beacons, whose unknown source engenders the fables that, since earliest childhood, have nourished me without consoling me.

Here, nothing grows and nothing shrinks. The belfry clock remains in neutral, midday or midnight, how should I know. The

chacun, une saison et n'en changent plus: côte à côte les uns sont couverts de fruits, les autres de neige. Le printemps coexiste avec un automne aviné et la femme aux seins lourds, aux yeux clairs et rieurs, jouant les rôles de servante, ne vieillira jamais.

Ici, plus de ménage, ni de marché ni d'hôpital, adieu béquilles et pansements, paniers à provisions, temple de l'esclavage, ni les congrès, ni la messe, ni canons, ni chars, ni tombeaux, ni l'heure de la soupe, ni l'heure de mourir, ni l'école, ni l'église, ni le bordel, ni les petits malins, ni les grands magasins. Allez au diable, peste de l'habitude, horribles riens de tous nos jours!

Ici, dans l'étendue redoutable et frémissante des coulisses – vraies et fausses comme l'Histoire –, les habitants qui vont et viennent sans se connaître, occupés à des jeux ridicules, à des crimes incompréhensibles et sacrés, portent les vêtements de tous les pays, de tous les âges – et je suis leur contemporain.

On me dit, mais je ne l'ai jamais vu, que, dans cet empire opulent et dérisoire, il y a des lieux cachés où, pareils aux femmes de Barbe-Bleue pendues dans l'armoire interdite, sont rangés tous les personnages dont nous ne sommes que les ombres, prêts à s'ébrouer au premier signal du régisseur et à monter en scène, selon la suprême ordonnance du programme, dans une réitération furibonde.

C'est que s'affirme ici, contre les désastres du feu, de la guerre et de l'eau, la toute-puissance du Texte, fixé en lettres et en images, sur les feuilles des grands livres, où les rumeurs du parler des peuples, conservées dans les herbiers de l'écriture, se taisent pour se maintenir. S'il est des jours où luit le miroitement des rayons sur l'océan, si les amoureux échangent des sanglots pour des baisers sans fin, si les conspirateurs, fourbissant leurs armes dans les tavernes, feignent de boire dans des gobelets de carton – quoi qu'il arrive, je sais que tout est d'abord désigné et inscrit –, avant d'apparaître sous les projecteurs et que rien de ce qui fait semblant de vivre et de mourir n'échappe aux plus fragiles et aux plus minces des supports: la feuille imprimée, les panneaux du peintre, la grille ailée des musiciens.

Souvent des cloches, lourdes ou grêles, parfois le sifflement d'une locomotive à vapeur, un gong, un clairon nasillard, un glissando de harpe, le roulement d'un tambour voilé, s'échelonnent du proche au lointain, rendant le silence et l'obscurité plus profonds encore et la lumière plus glauque, car le prélude est fait pour être deviné plutôt que compris, pour créer une attente curieuse ou angoissée, selon les rites de l'orage, avant que le

trees have each adopted a season and no longer change: side by side, some bear fruit and others snow. Springtime co-exists with the mellow intoxication of autumn and the heavy-breasted woman with bright laughing eyes, who plays the servants' parts, will never age.

Here, no more housework, no more trips to the market, no more hospital, farewell crutches and bandages, shopping baskets, temple of slavery, neither congresses nor mass, no guns, no tanks, no tombs, neither time for supper nor time for death, no school, no church, no brothel, neither little sneaks nor big stores. The devil with you, cursed habit, fearsome void of all our days!

Here, in the frightening fragile space of the wings – as true and as false as History – the local inhabitants, who come and go without recognising each other, engaged in trivial pursuits, in sacred and incomprehensible crimes, wear garments deriving from all countries and all ages – and I am their contemporary.

They say, although I would not know, that in this opulent and derisory empire there lie hidden places, where, like Bluebeard's wives hung up in the secret cupboard, are stacked all the characters of which we are but the shadows, ready to scramble at the first sign from the production manager, and to come on stage, according to the overriding directions of the programme.

For here is affirmed, despite the disasters of fire, flood and war, the omnipotence of the Text, fixed in words and images on the leaves of the great books, where the rumblings of popular speech, conserved in the herbaria of writing, seek silence in order still to speak. If there are days when shimmering rays gleam on the ocean, when lovers exchange their sighs for never-ending kisses, if conspirators sharpening their daggers in taverns make as to drink out of cardboard goblets – whatever happens, I know that everything has first been planned out and set down – before appearing under the spotlights, and that nothing that makes any semblance of living and dying can escape those most slender and fragile vehicles, the written page, the painter's panel, the winged bars of the composer.

Often the sound of bells, light and clear or dull and dark, sometimes the hissing of a steam-engine, a gong, a snuffling bugle call, the glissando of a harp, a muffled drum-roll, stretch out at intervals from near to far, increasing the depth of the silence and darkness and the murkiness of the light, for the prelude is intended to be divined rather than comprehended, to create the curiosity or anxiety of anticipation, following the ritual of the storm, before the

tonnerre ne s'approche et que la foudre, dans le plein accomplissement de l'orchestre, ne nous apporte enfin la délivrance, le châtiment des innocents.

Peu après, éclate la Fête.

D'abord viennent les balayeurs, soldats de plume et de paille, aux gestes unis en cadence, troupe aussi nombreuse qu'une harde en forêt, aussi policée qu'un ballet de cour.

Alors les ténèbres des décors s'éclaircissent peu à peu: quelques points çà et là, puis d'autres, beaucoup d'autres et la scène s'embrase en retard, comme si la lumière était plus vaste que les lampes.

Ensuite le corps des balayeurs se disperse ou plutôt je passe au travers de ces taciturnes fantômes et la représentation peut, enfin, commencer.

L'innombrable théâtre vient à moi, qui suis seul dans la salle. Souvent aussi, c'est moi qui vais à sa rencontre. Je m'avance, écartant le murmure des acteurs et découvrant les scènes successives, qui s'illuminent au fur et à mesure de ma promenade inquiète et ravie.

Il n'est pas rare qu'au détour d'une rue pavée de dalles à l'antique, j'aperçoive, assise nue et jouant de la flûte à deux becs, une jeune musicienne dont les contours délicieux sont à peine ombrés (car elle vient, pour commencer à vivre, de se détacher de la pierre), et, quelques pas plus loin, sur un fond de ténèbres fumeuses et sifflantes une longue femme hagarde qui cherche à effacer sur sa main une tache indélébile. L'une est mon loisir, ma volupté, l'autre ma souveraine, ma mère, mon amante impitoyable.

Mais mon propre rôle n'est pas seulement d'être le spectateur. Je gravis parfois les degrés jusqu'à la scène, où je me sens transfiguré. Je joue, je vocifère et tantôt je déclame l'ardente conjuration, la plainte sans espoir, l'adieu cruel, prenant à témoin les lumignons des corridors et les toiles d'araignées, tantôt j'apprends à me taire, roulant des yeux sous mes sourcils et méditant une vengeance assassine contre un ennemi dont je ne sais rien, sinon qu'il veut ma perte et la disparition de tout ce que j'aime.

Aussi quand les Puissances invisibles qui me gouvernent, bien en deçà des enfers, me disent de tuer, alors je tue!

J'ai, pour cela, un arsenal complet d'armes de diverses sortes et de multiples provenances: sabres de bois, sabres de samouraï, fusils à pierre, à tromblon, au canon scié, des pistolets militaires, des revolvers de western, des couteaux larges et longs comme des

thunder draws closer, and before the lightning, in the crowning consummation of the orchestra, finally offers us deliverance, the castigation of the innocents.

Shortly after, the festivities break out.

First come the cleaners, plumed straw soldiers, their gestures in unison, in tune with the rhythm, numerous as a pack of hounds in the forest, as perfectly regulated as a court ballet.

Now the darkness of the décor is gradually lightened: a few spots here and there, then more, many more, and the stage acquires a retarded brilliance, as though the light were larger than the lamps.

Then the troupe of cleaners disperses, or rather I pass through these mute phantoms and the performance can, at last, begin.

The numerous theatre comes towards me, alone in the auditorium. But often I also move towards it. I go forward, sweeping aside the mumbling of the actors and discovering the scenes one after another, as they light up in the course of my anguished, fascinated ambulation.

Quite often, turning the corner of a street paved with the flagstones of antiquity, I glimpse a young woman playing the pipes of Pan, sitting naked, the perfect lines of her body hardly shaded in (for she has just escaped the stone to start to live), and, a few steps farther on, against a back-cloth of hissing, smoky shadows, I come across a tall, haggard woman, trying to rub from her hand an indelible stain. The one is my leisure, my pleasure, the other my ruler, my mother, my pitiless lover.

But my own part is not just that of the spectator. Sometimes I climb the steps which lead to the stage, where I feel myself transfigured. I play, I rant, and sometimes I declaim the ardent oath, the hopeless plaint, the cruel farewell, taking as witnesses the pitiful lights in the corridors and the spiders' webs, and sometimes I learn to keep my peace, rolling my eyeballs under my bushy brows and dreaming of murderous revenge on an enemy quite unknown to me, except in so far as he seeks my downfall and the loss of all that is dear to me.

And so, when the invisible Powers which govern me, clearly situated on this side of the Underworld, tell me to kill, then I kill.

For this I have a whole arsenal of weapons of various sorts, deriving from diverse sources: wooden swords, Samurai sabres, flintlocks and firelocks, sawn-off shotguns, army pistols and cowboy colts, knives as long and as broad as cake-slices.

What happens? This is the way it is: my victims rise up at a given point, more menacing than the hangman, but already condemned

pelles à tarte.

Ce qui se passe? Voici: mes victimes se dressent à point nommé, plus menaçantes que le bourreau, mais déjà condamnées, le cœur désigné par un point rouge – et déjà elles s'écroulent, un centième de seconde *avant* que je n'aie tiré ou que je n'aie frappé.

En vérité, sous l'effet d'une fatalité dont je ne suis que l'exécutant (ou le prétexte), elles s'écroulent sans un cri, sans un râle et un petit nuage s'élève du sol sous la chute des corps, lourds comme ils sont et chargés d'oripeaux, de vêtements chamarrés, de baudriers bien garnis, parfois de sceptres et de couronnes. Les balayeurs aussitôt, sur la pointe des pieds, enlèvent ces vestiges et vont sans bruit les ranger plus loin dans le vestiaire vertigineux.

Ailleurs, sous un balcon chargé de glycines en papier, il est arrivé que je m'égare au milieu d'un grand salon éclairé de lustres en cristal, où des rentiers louis-philippards en costumes aux tons délicats: puce, chamois, beige, gris perle, robes en cloche, bijoux éblouissants, échangeaient de fades propos. Mais au moindre souffle, au revoir! Les visages s'effacèrent, les perruques blondes, les barbes noires ont jonché le sol. Tout s'effondrait, les vêtements étaient vides.

Mais encore, qui pourrait rendre le pas, qui s'envole et retombe mollement – si lourd, accompagné par les ictus des basses, si léger dans l'escalade aiguë des clarinettes –, de ce Pierrot classique, ravivé par l'imprévu des dissonances, le même peut-être, qui, de face, autrefois, immobile et l'œil fixe, sous le nom de Gilles, trahissait l'hébétude et la fatigue de savoir que tout est vain?

Explose alors une gerbe de fleurs jamais vues, tisons assourdis sous la cendre. Oui, sur les murs de mon théâtre, tachés de rouille, griffés de rayures à peine discernables et de «bonommes» en graffiti, des corolles bariolées font alterner ou se joindre un bleu promis plutôt que tenu, le vert puisé dans une mémoire profonde, le violet qu'il faut imaginer pour y croire. Avec les senteurs qu'ils suggèrent, ces pétales poudrés de pollen éclatent comme des sons, comme des cris et je n'ai pas à les cueillir, car ils sont, en moi, une réponse possible et victorieuse au blond sapin capitonné qui nous attend.

Arrive, à ce moment, une fanfare citadine qui marque le pas d'une petite troupe en marche. Les buffleteries, les larges ceintures de soie sur des redingotes rebondies, les manches de dentelles, les visages surmontés de chapeaux enrubannés surgissent dans la nuit (on les distingue à peine à la lueur des lanternes).

Après leur passage et le bruit des bottes qui décroît, porté par

to death, their hearts indicated by a red spot – and they drop already, a hundredth of a second *before* before I shoot or stab.

In truth, functioning in terms of a fatality of which I am but the executor (or the pretext), they drop without a cry, without a death-rattle, and a little cloud rises from the earth as the bodies fall, heavy with their own weight, and burdened with tinselled tawdry braided costumes, heavy bandoliers, sometimes even with sceptres and crowns. The cleaners, on tiptoe, remove these remnants in a trice, and silently go to hang them elsewhere in the vertiginous wardrobe.

Elsewhere, beneath a balcony laden with paper wisteria, I have sometimes been lost in the middle of a large salon lit by crystal chandeliers, in which rich bourgeois of the age of Louis-Philippe, dressed in delicate tones – puce, fawn, beige, pearl-grey, crinolines, with dazzling jewellery – were engaged in banal conversation. But, at the slightest breath, goodbye! The faces disappeared, the blond wigs and black beards suddenly littered the floor. Everything would crumble, the clothes would be empty.

And yet, who could render the tread, gently taking off and falling – so heavily when accompanied by the violent interruptions of the basses, so lightly to the rising crescendo of the clarinets – of that classic Pierrot, brought back to life by unexpected dissonances, perhaps even the very one who, long ago, under the name of Gilles, disclosed, full-face, motionless and with staring gaze, the stupefied weariness of knowing that all is vanity?

Then there is a burst, a spray, of unimaginable flowers, brands half-sleeping beneath the ashes. Yes, on the rust-stained walls of my theatre, scarred by hardly visible scratches and crude graffiti, multi-coloured petals create contrasts and combinations of a blue which is rather hinted at than solid, green drawn from the depths of memory, violet which has to be imagined to be believed. With their suggested scents these petals dusted with pollen burst like sounds and cries, and I do not need to pluck them, for they represent, within me, a possible triumphant response to the plush whitewood which awaits us all.

At that precise moment a town band arrives, beating out the step for a small troupe of marchers. The leather gear, the broad silken sashes on bulging frock-coats, the lace cuffs, the faces topped by ribbonned hats, loom up out of the darkness (hardly distinguishable in the lantern light).

After they have gone, as the sound of their boots on the pavement recedes, the noise carried by the sleeping canals, everything returns to thick darkness. Then there comes another

l'écho des canaux dormants, tout retombe dans une épaisse obscurité. S'avance alors une autre figure de femme, grande et mince, elle aussi, mais ses longs vêtements de bure, sa coiffe de nonne et la rigueur anguleuse de ses gestes sont inscrits dans une géométrie savante, soigneusement dissimulée. Elle élève au-dessus de sa tête une torche de résine dont la flamme toute droite l'éclaire d'un seul côté. Elle se penche et découvre à ses pieds, sur la paille, le corps ridé de Job, reconnaissable à sa maigreur extrême.

À peine cette vision a-t-elle tremblé dans mon regard, la voici qui vacille et s'éteint. J'entends un déclic mécanique aussitôt suivi du grignotement saccadé d'un film qui défile. Surgit la vision grisâtre d'une banlieue pauvre de New York, où se disputent des enfants déguenillés et où s'avance en sautillant un petit homme qui fait des moulinets avec sa canne.

La moue qui agite sa moustache noire, l'équilibre menacé de son chapeau melon, tout exprime à la fois une mélancolie sans remède et la dérision qui venge le malheur. Soudain, il se retourne et s'éloigne. Il court vite, chevauchant un énorme sillon dans un champ si monotone et si vaste qu'au loin déjà il n'est plus qu'un point, le signe de la fin des temps.

Surtout, ne venez pas me réveiller! Ne marchez pas sur l'or factice de mes spectacles! De ce côté-ci où je demeure, solitaire et oublié comme si déjà m'abritait mon sépulcre, je vois les temples superposés dont les degrés fatiguent les géants, tandis qu'un peu plus loin, s'assombrit l'horizon orageux où des cavaliers au manteau déployé par le vent galopent sur une route en lacets et que les feuilles mortes s'éparpillent dans l'air, accompagnées d'oiseaux qui sont les traits mêmes de l'idéogramme vertical, distincts et nets sur la rondeur de l'astre rouge…

Dans mon théâtre se succèdent, à la vitesse du rêve, un faux malade qui crache du vrai sang et qui, pour nous sauver, agonise dans son rire, la grâce divine des voix et des violons, entraînée vers la mort par une main de pierre, au glas répété des timbales, un ascenseur qui ne cesse d'aller et venir entre les sous-sols et les cintres, faisant descendre sur des nuages les dieux arrogants de l'Olympe et monter des enfers provinciaux une famille en noir qui cherche son auteur.

Pardonnez-moi! J'ai eu parfois l'audace impie (sans prévenir l'Econome ni les machinistes) d'introduire en fraude, dans le magasin général, quelques menus accessoires (par exemple un trou de serrure, un guichet d'ancienne gare, des pupitres où nul ne chante) et de vous passer, comme une maladie, quelques-uns de

female figure, also tall and slender, but her long coarse woollen garb, her nun's coiffe, and the angular rigidity of her gestures are incorporated into a carefully dissimulated but knowing geometric structure. She holds above her head a torch whose vertical flame illuminates her on one side only. She bends down, and finds, at her feet, on the straw, the wrinkled corpse of Job, recognisable by his extreme thinness.

Hardly has this vision flickered before my gaze, but it becomes hazy and disappears. I hear a mechanical clicking noise, immediately followed by the uneven whirring of a film being shown. Up comes the murky grey vision of a poor suburb in New York, with scrapping, ragged children, and, jerkily advancing, a little man twirling his stick.

The forward thrust of the lips which makes his black moustache twitch, the threatening equilibrium of his bowler hat, all expresses both an irremediable sense of sadness and that derision which is a form of revenge against misfortune. Suddenly, he turns round and goes away. He runs quickly, jumping over an enormous furrow in a field so broad and so monotonous that in the distance he is already no more than a spot, the sign of the end of time.

Whatever you do, do not come to wake me! Do not walk on the fool's gold of my performances! On this side, where I remain, solitary and forgotten as though I were already sheltered in my sepulchre, I see layered temples with steps to weary giants, whereas, a little further on there darkens the stormy horizon where cavaliers with capes streaming in the wind gallop along a hairpin road and dead leaves scatter in the air, accompanied by birds whose lines form the vertical ideogram, sharp and clear against the red disk of the sun...

In my theatre come, one after the other, a man feigning sickness who spits real blood, and who, for our salvation, dies laughing, the divine grace of voices and violins, drawn towards death by hand of stone, to the repeated death-knell beaten out on kettle-drums, a lift incessantly coming and going from beneath the stage to the flies, bringing down, perched on clouds, the arrogant gods of Olympus and raising up from the provincial underworld a family dressed in black in search of its author.

Forgive me! I have sometimes had the impious audacity to sneak into the props room (without warning the Financial Manager or the technicians) various small accessories (for example a keyhole, an old station ticket office, a music-stand at which no one sings), and to pass on, like a contagious illness, some of my animated dreams:

mes songes animés: la confusion des mots (ce masque d'un profond silence), la détresse de ceux qui n'auront jamais le droit d'être vus de nos yeux, la foule qui se referme sur les amants pour les dévorer dans un souterrain, le pernicieux sommeil qui lâche la bride à nos monstres – et ce pressentiment dont je ne suis pas digne et que nul ne fait qu'entrevoir.

Adieu! J'ai trop parlé, mais je suis libre…Je fais ce que je veux avec ce que je crois savoir et ma mémoire fouille sans fin dans le monceau des choses que j'ignore.

Encore quelques enjambées dans cette course haletante vers le secret qui se dérobe (dont j'entends le rire d'enfant, dont je perçois la lueur dansante) et je parviendrai à retrouver, dans ce théâtre d'ombres, ce que peut-être j'ai su dans un autre temps, sous une autre enveloppe et que je cherche sans relâche et que j'ai oublié.

the confusion of words (that mask of deep silence), the distress of those who will never have the right to be seen by our eyes, the crowd which closes in on lovers to devour them underground, the pernicious sleep which unleashes our monsters – and that presentiment of which I am unworthy and which no one can do more than glimpse.

Farewell! I have talked too much, but I am free...I do what I will with what I think I know, and my memory scavenges incessantly in the heap of things I do not know.

A few more paces in that breathless race towards the ever elusive secret (whose childlike laughter I hear, and whose dancing glimmer I perceive), and I shall manage to rediscover in this shadow theatre, what perhaps I knew in another time, in a different skin, and seek relentlessly and have forgotten.

FIGURES OF MOVEMENT
LES FIGURES DU MOUVEMENT
(1987)

Les figures de mouvement
(sur douze dessins de Hans Hartnung)

I

Sur le théâtre de ce monde
décors immenses
bruits et couleurs
nous les vivants
nous les objets
nous sommes les figures
la trace et le sillage
des mouvements qui nous emportent
et nous animent
par le dedans

II

L'aigu
est lancé,
au-delà de tout espace
concevable,
par un geste
qui est l'ombre amassée
toujours plus noire
dans l'épaisseur.

III

Parfois
je dormais
enroulé sur moi-même
lové
les plumes repliées
parce que l'origine
est ainsi
dans sa palpitation aveugle
avant de donner vie
à l'être qui refuse
et tremble encore
de peur.

Figures of Movement
(after twelve drawings by Hans Hartnung)

I

On the theatre of this world
enormous sets
sounds and colours
we the living
we the objects
we are the figures
the trace and wake
of the movements which sweep us away
and buoy us up
from within

II

Acute
the angle is hurled
beyond all conceivable
space
by a gesture
which is gathered shade
ever darker
in depth.

III

Sometimes
I would sleep
wound up in myself
coiled
feathers folded
for thus
is the origin
in its blind palpitation
before giving birth
to the reluctant being
which quivers still
with fear.

IV

Ce treillis embrouillé
c'est la prison
que j'ai créée à ma mesure
pour que la seule lueur
le cri
me délivre.

V

Avant tout départ
je m'envole
par le désir.
A ma lourdeur j'oppose
un refus qui exige
et qui brûle
pour ma cendre.

VI

Ce qui est visible
est double:
tout reflet
que caresse amoureuse
la main
se détache sur la pâleur
de son ombre.

VII

L'Un
qui enfante le Multiple
s'étonne d'avoir soudain
tant d'ailes
pour un seul élan
dans le lointain
inépuisable.

IV

This tangled trellis
is the prison
I fashioned to my size
for the only gleam
the cry
to offer deliverance.

V

Before each departure
I take wing
through desire.
To my weight I oppose
a refusal which insists
and which burns
for my ashes.

VI

All that we see
is two-faced
every reflection
lovingly touched
by the hand
stands out against the pallor
of its shadow.

VII

The One
engendering the Multiple
is surprised suddenly
to have so many wings
for a single flight
into the inexhaustible
distance.

VIII

Le pressentiment
qui nous sauve
et souvent nous ravit
jusqu'au vertige
c'est de savoir
que le possible
n'a pas de fin.

IX

Feindre de fuir
dans tous les sens
et se retrouver réuni
dans une ligne,
sortir du tumulte
et des visages de la vie
pour retomber
dans un repos
chargé de sens
c'est changer la musique
en un regard
silencieux.

X

À qui éprouve
dans son être
le mouvement
mourir n'a pas de sens
car sous nos masques
nous ressemblons
à ce qui bouge
et se divise
pour se refondre
et s'égarer.

VIII

The saving
foreboding
which often enraptures
till the head swims
is knowing
there is no end to
the possible.

IX

Feigning flight
in all directions
finding oneself contained
in a line
escaping the tumult
and the faces of life
falling back
into a repose
laden with meaning
is to transform music
into a silent
gaze.

X

For him who feels
movement
within his being
dying has no sense
for beneath our masks
we resemble
what moves
and splits
to be re-fused
and go astray.

XI

La force qui s'élève de la terre
devient cet arbre
ou cet oiseau
ou ce volcan.
L'eau qui s'amasse
ou qui retombe et s'éparpille
devient l'averse
ou bien le fleuve
ou bien la mer.
Le temps qui s'étire et s'étire
devient constellation.
Une pensée obscure
qui s'appelle l'aurore
devient un œil
complice d'une main
à la recherche du secret.

XII

Ailleurs
plus loin
que la lumière
et ses ténèbres
dans un futur
prédestiné
et peut-être déjà
révolu
règne la roue
inexplicable
de ce qui est
ou qui n'est plus.

XI

The force which rises from the earth
becomes this tree
or that bird
or this volcano.
The water which collects
or which falls and sprinkles
becomes the shower
or the river
or even the sea.
Time which stretches and stretches
becomes constellation.
An obscure thought
known as dawn
becomes an eye
accomplice of a hand
in search of the secret.

XII

Elsewhere
beyond
light
and its shadows
in a future
predestined
and perhaps already
past
reigns the
inexplicable wheel
of what is
or what is no more.

Bloodaxe Contemporary French Poets

Series Editors: Timothy Mathews & Michael Worton

FRENCH-ENGLISH BILINGUAL EDITIONS

1: **Yves Bonnefoy:** *On the Motion and Immobility of Douve /
Du mouvement et de l'immobilité de Douve*
Trans. Galway Kinnell. Introduction: Timothy Mathews. £7.95

2: **René Char:** *The Dawn Breakers / Les Matinaux*
Trans. & intr. Michael Worton. [out of print]

3: **Henri Michaux:** *Spaced, Displaced / Déplacements Dégagements*
Trans. David & Helen Constantine. Introduction: Peter Broome.
[out of print]

4: **Aimé Césaire:** *Notebook of a Return to My Native Land /
Cahier d'un retour au pays natal*
Trans. & intr. Mireille Rosello (with Annie Pritchard). £12

5: **Philippe Jaccottet:** *Under Clouded Skies / Beauregard
Pensées sous les nuages / Beauregard*
Trans. David Constantine & Mark Treharne.
Introduction: Mark Treharne. £12

6: **Paul Éluard:** *Unbroken Poetry II / Poésie ininterrompue II*
Trans. Gilbert Bowen. Introduction: Jill Lewis. [out of print]

7: **André Frénaud:** *Rome the Sorceress / La Sorcière de Rome*
Trans. Keith Bosley. Introduction: Peter Broome. £8.95

8: **Gérard Macé:** *Wood Asleep / Bois dormant*
Trans. David Kelley. Introduction: Jean-Pierre Richard. £8.95

9: **Guillevic:** *Carnac*
Trans. John Montague. Introduction: Stephen Romer. £12

10: **Salah Stétié:** *Cold Water Shielded: Selected Poems*
Trans. & intr. Michael Bishop. £9.95

'Bloodaxe's Contemporary French Poets series could not have arrived
at a more opportune time, and I cannot remember any translation
initiative in the past thirty years that has been more ambitious or
more coherently planned in its attempt to bring French poetry
across the Channel and the Atlantic. Under the editorship of
Timothy Mathews and Michael Worton, the series has a clear for-
mat and an even clearer sense of mission' – MALCOLM BOWIE, *TLS*

9 781852 240998